Contents

CW01655897

Introduction

Problem solving

Following the introduction of the **National Numeracy Strategy *Framework for Teaching Mathematics***, overall standards of numeracy in primary schools have been steadily rising. However, of the five strands covered by the Framework, there is one which teachers often find harder to integrate into their lessons – solving problems. The *Problem Solving* series of books is designed to help you meet the objectives of this solving problems strand. The books provide suggestions on how to incorporate opportunities for children to develop more sophisticated problem-solving strategies into your teaching.

Solving problems is at the heart of mathematical learning and should be integrated throughout the other strands where it can be placed in context. It is vital that children recognise that methods as well as answers are important. They should use their knowledge in other areas of mathematics to interpret problems and check that their methods and answers are reasonable. *Problem Solving* aims to encourage children to extend their individual thinking skills to make sense of problems and identify the operations needed to solve them. However, they will still need help to develop the skills needed to explain and demonstrate their methods, as well as to explore the reasons for any wrong answers.

Problem Solving, therefore, provides detailed notes for the teacher on how to model and present the problems and puzzles. The photocopiable pupil pages contain simple text, so difficulty with reading will not preclude participation in mathematical activities. The teacher's notes often give more background to the task, allowing you to give support to the children who need it.

Planning and teaching

Each *Problem Solving* unit has been carefully matched to the **National Numeracy Strategy *Sample Medium Term Plans***, so as to reduce the time needed for planning. Termly matching charts are provided to enable you to dovetail the relevant *Problem Solving* Unit into your planning, whatever materials you are using to deliver the Daily Maths Lesson. There are 36 units within each book, each providing five problems. These can be used flexibly as one activity per day, or presented altogether at the end of each week or topic.

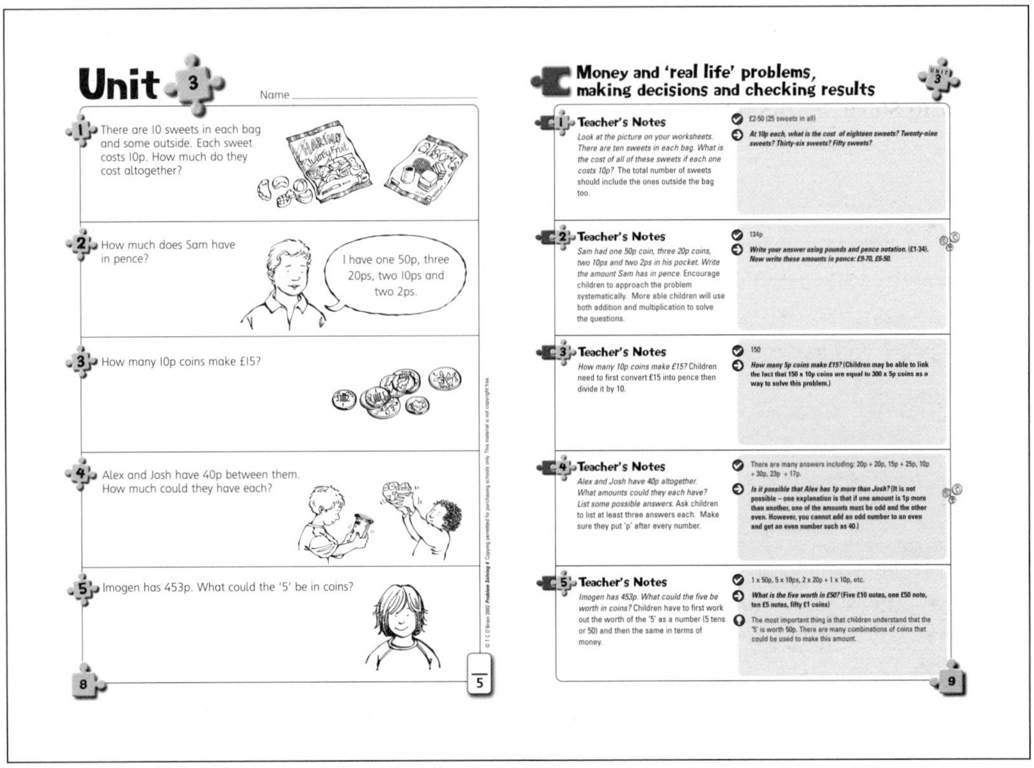

Unit 3 Name

1 There are 10 sweets in each bag and some outside. Each sweet costs 10p. How much do they cost altogether?

2 How much does Sam have in pence?

I have one 50p, three 20ps, two 10ps and two 2ps.

3 How many 10p coins make £15?

4 Alex and Josh have 40p between them. How much could they have each?

5 Imogen has 453p. What could the '5' be in coins?

8

5

© T C O'Brien 2002 *Problem Solving 4*. Copying permitted for purchasing schools only. This material is not copyright free.

Money and 'real life' problems, making decisions and checking results

Unit 3

1 Teacher's Notes

Look at the picture on your worksheets. There are ten sweets in each bag. What is the cost of all of these sweets if each one costs 10p? The total number of sweets should include the ones outside the bag too.

£2·50 (25 sweets in all)

At 10p each, what is the cost of eighteen sweets? Twenty-nine sweets? Thirty-six sweets? Fifty sweets?

2 Teacher's Notes

Sam had one 50p coin, three 20p coins, two 10ps and two 2ps in his pocket. Write the amount Sam has in pence. Encourage children to approach the problem systematically. More able children will use both addition and multiplication to solve the questions.

134p

Write your answer using pounds and pence notation.* (£1·34). *Now write these amounts in pence: £9·70, £6·50.

3 Teacher's Notes

How many 10p coins make £15? Children need to first convert £15 into pence then divide it by 10.

150

***How many 5p coins make £15?* (Children may be able to link the fact that 150 x 10p coins are equal to 300 x 5p coins as a way to solve this problem.)**

4 Teacher's Notes

Alex and Josh have 40p altogether. What amounts could they each have? List some possible answers. Ask children to list at least three answers each. Make sure they put 'p' after every number.

There are many answers including: 20p + 20p, 15p + 25p, 10p + 30p, 23p + 17p.

***Is it possible that Alex has 1p more than Josh?* (It is not possible – one explanation is that if one amount is 1p more than another, one of the amounts must be odd and the other even. However, you cannot add an odd number to an even and get an even number such as 40.)**

5 Teacher's Notes

Imogen has 453p. What could the five be worth in coins? Children have to first work out the worth of the '5' as a number (5 tens or 50) and then the same in terms of money.

1 x 50p, 5 x 10ps, 2 x 20p + 1 x 10p, etc.

***What is the five worth in £50?* (Five £10 notes, one £50 note, ten £5 notes, fifty £1 coins)**

The most important thing is that children understand that the '5' is worth 50p. There are many combinations of coins that could be used to make this amount.

9

The notes on the right-hand page of each unit provide all the information you need to use the sheets. The 'Teacher's Notes' section explains the problem, tells you of any preparation or special equipment you will need, and suggests ways in which the problem can be presented to the children. Suggested words which you may wish to use have been italicised, but you can, of course, adapt these. Alongside the 'Teacher's Notes' you will also find the answers and an activity which can be used as a follow up. These follow-up activities can be used in whole class teaching or as an extension for more able children. Some may also be used to form the basis of a homework investigation. There are also occasional tips. These range from alternative methods to support children who are struggling, to ways to present children's results.

Resources

Where resources other than the photocopiable recording sheet are required, these are mainly materials which are generally available in the classroom. The use of other equipment has been kept to a minimum. Any additional materials required are indicated by the following icons.

number cards, interlocking cubes, dice, counters, coins, calculator, protractor, written answer required, extra paper required, coloured pencils, ruler, 3-d shapes, 2-d shapes, place-value cards

Differentiation

Open-ended problems are used wherever possible, enabling each child to work at his or her own level of attainment. Added flexibility is given by the format of the pupil page. Many of the problems can be answered orally. Where a written answer is required, or in cases where the pupil page provides additional essential information, the icon indicates this on the teacher's page. The activities suggested on the teacher's page can often be adapted to suit the needs of your class, or tailored for individual children.

Working together

Throughout the book children are encouraged to solve problems by working collaboratively. There is an emphasis on practical activities for the whole class and for work in groups and pairs. The children's learning is continually reinforced by activities such as explaining methods to a partner, or setting problems for their partner to solve. In this way, children are encouraged to go beyond completing the activity, and also to reflect on their methods.

Assessment

Space is provided on each pupil page (—/5) to record the children's achievement if you choose to allocate marks. You will need to decide upon your own marking scheme as totals for each unit will vary depending on how and whether you ask children to record their work for each problem.

Two recording sheets are provided at the back of this book:

- Individual record sheet
- Class record sheet.

The 'Individual record sheet' may be photocopied for each child. Space is provided for you to record comments on the child's achievement in each unit. The 'Class record sheet' lists the Units and can be used to summarise the performance of the class as a whole. It is designed to provide an overall picture of the children's achievements, and help to identify any areas which may benefit from further reinforcement. These sheets can be used in your own record keeping, or passed to a receiving teacher at the end of the year.

Unit 1

Name ______________________

1 What is the figure 6 worth in this number?

463

2 Make a 3-digit number as close as possible to 1000.

3 Imagine a class of 20 children. Estimate the number of pockets they have altogether.

4 Enter this number into your calculator.

Two thousand two hundred and two

5 Make up a story using the number 1198.

Place-value, ordering and rounding

1 Teacher's Notes

What is the figure six in the number four hundred and sixty-three worth? Check that children understand the question. The number can be broken down into: 400 + 60 + 3.

6 tens or 60.

What is the three in each of these numbers worth? Thirty-five; nine hundred and thirty-eight; three thousand, nine hundred and eighty-two; four thousand, nine hundred and fifty-three.

2 Teacher's Notes

Choose from the cards to make a 3-digit number as close as possible to one thousand. As there are four numbers to choose from children need to work out the best three and arrange them to make the largest 3-digit number.

873

Which number is as far as possible from 1000? (137)

3 Teacher's Notes

Imagine a class of twenty children. Which of these is the best guess at the number of pockets they will have altogether? a 5. b 20. c 70. d 250. Explain your answer. Children may count their pockets and find an average of 2 to 3 per child. They should multiply this by 20.

The exact answer would depend on the children, but the most likely answer is 70.

How can you decide on your answer without counting all the pockets? Would you get a different answer if everyone was ready to go out for play/to do PE etc? Why?

4 Teacher's Notes

Enter this number in your calculator: two thousand two hundred and two. Ask the children to re-write the number on paper and check they have it right.

2202

Enter these numbers in your calculator: one thousand and seven, two hundred and eight, four thousand two hundred. Can you enter a number larger than 2202 into your calculator, using the same digits?

5 Teacher's Notes

Make up a real life story involving the number one thousand one hundred and ninety-eight. Encourage children to start with a number that is bigger or smaller than 1198.

There are many possible stories, for example, 1200 people were to attend a championship tennis match. However, two of them got the flu and could not come. So, only 1198 showed up.

Make up a multiplication question where the answer is 1198.

Unit 2

Name ______________________

1 How many more counters do you need to make 50?

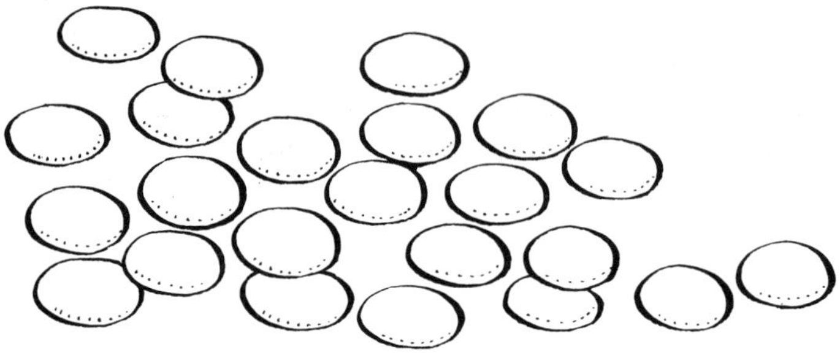

2 Alison is counting backwards in tens, starting on 118. She won't go past 70. How many numbers will she say?

3 Complete this sequence.

657 ____ 857 957 ____ 1157 ____

4 Show how you would add 60, 20 and 70.

5 How many ways can you make 100 with these numbers?

62	**27**	**23**	**75**
7	**60**	**20**	**10**
55	**25**	**38**	**5**
15	**80**	**45**	**40**

5

Understanding addition and subtraction

1 Teacher's Notes

Look at the picture. How many more counters are needed to make fifty altogether? Some children may expect to use real counters to work out the answer but encourage them to work it out without counters.

27 more counters are needed.

If you had two hundred and thirty counters, how many would you need to make five hundred? If you have two thousand, three hundred counters how many would you need to make five thousand? How can you use the previous answer to help you?

Ask children how they worked out the answer. This question lends itself to a 'counting on' approach, e.g. *You started with twenty-three. Seven more gets you to thirty and another twenty gets you to fifty.* You might like to reinforce this with similar examples, using a number line to help.

2 Teacher's Notes

Alison is going to count backwards in tens. She will start with one hundred and eighteen, but she won't count past seventy. How many numbers will Alison say? Children will find it helpful to write down each number they say.

118, 108, 98, 88, 78 = 5 numbers

***Start at ninety-four and count up six steps of ten. Where will you finish?* (154)**

One method which will help children visualise the steps is to use a number line and count the jumps needed.

3 Teacher's Notes

Complete the sequence on your worksheets to fill in the missing numbers. At the start, remind children what a sequence is: it is a pattern of numbers where the operation performed on each number to find the next is the same each time.

757, 1057, 1257

The sequence involves adding on a fixed amount each time. How much is added each time?* (100) *Create another sequence adding on a fixed amount each time – ask a partner to write the next step.

4 Teacher's Notes

How would you add these three numbers? Use jottings to show the way you would work this out in your head. Which numbers would you add first? Would you use any smaller addition facts to help you?

Children may use 7 + 6 + 2 = 15 to help them. They may count on in tens from 70 (the largest of the three numbers) making jottings as they go to keep track. They many imagine a number line or number grid as a way of aiding their counting on. Give them time to listen to each other's methods and evaluate the suitability of each.

Ask the children to make choices about suitable methods for other additions of three numbers, e.g. (17, 5, 3); (15, 14, 6); (20, 13, 80). It is important that children learn to choose the best method, according to the numbers involved.

5 Teacher's Notes

Look at your worksheet. How many different ways can you make 100 with this set of numbers? Ask children to make at least five combinations.

Answers include: 55 + 45, 75 + 25, 62 + 38, 20 + 80, 60 + 40, 60 + 25 + 15, 62 + 15 + 23, 15 + 45 + 40, 75 + 10 + 15, 60 + 10 + 23 + 7; 27 + 25 + 38 + 10, 55 + 25 + 15 + 5.

Is it possible to add five of the numbers together to make one hundred?

Unit 3

Name ____________________

1 There are 10 sweets in each bag and some outside. Each sweet costs 10p. How much do they cost altogether?

2 How much does Sam have in pence?

3 How many 10p coins make £15?

4 Alex and Josh have 40p between them. How much could they have each?

5 Imogen has 453p. What could the '5' be in coins?

/5

Money and 'real life' problems, making decisions and checking results

UNIT 3

1 Teacher's Notes

Look at the picture on your worksheets. There are ten sweets in each bag. What is the cost of all of these sweets if each one costs 10p? The total number of sweets should include the ones outside the bag too.

£2·50 (25 sweets in all)

At 10p each, what is the cost of eighteen sweets? Twenty-nine sweets? Thirty-six sweets? Fifty sweets?

2 Teacher's Notes

Sam had one 50p coin, three 20p coins, two 10ps and two 2ps in his pocket. Write the amount Sam has in pence. Encourage children to approach the problem systematically. More able children will use both addition and multiplication to solve the questions.

134p

Write your answer using pounds and pence notation.* (£1·34). *Now write these amounts in pence: £9·70, £6·50.

3 Teacher's Notes

How many 10p coins make £15? Children need to first convert £15 into pence then divide it by 10.

150

***How many 5p coins make £15?* (Children may be able to link the fact that 150 x 10p coins are equal to 300 x 5p coins as a way to solve this problem.)**

4 Teacher's Notes

Alex and Josh have 40p altogether. What amounts could they each have? List some possible answers. Ask children to list at least three answers each. Make sure they put 'p' after every number.

There are many answers including: 20p + 20p, 15p + 25p, 10p + 30p, 23p + 17p.

***Is it possible that Alex has 1p more than Josh?* (It is not possible – one explanation is that if one amount is 1p more than another, one of the amounts must be odd and the other even. However, you cannot add an odd number to an even and get an even number such as 40.)**

5 Teacher's Notes

Imogen has 453p. What could the five be worth in coins? Children have to first work out the worth of the '5' as a number (5 tens or 50) and then the same in terms of money.

1 x 50p, 5 x 10ps, 2 x 20p + 1 x 10p, etc.

***What is the five worth in £50?* (Five £10 notes, one £50 note, ten £5 notes, fifty £1 coins)**

The most important thing is that children understand that the '5' is worth 50p. There are many combinations of coins that could be used to make this amount.

Unit 4

Name ______________________

1 Estimate the length of your pencil ________ cm

Measure to check ________ cm

Is it longer or shorter than this pencil?

2 Draw Jamil's rectangle.

3 Estimate the length of this page ________ cm

Measure to check ________ cm

How close was your estimate?

4 Work in pairs. Estimate the length of your giant-sized step.

How can you measure it?

5 Draw a rectangle with a perimeter of 14 cm.

$\overline{}$ 5

Measures, including problems

1 Teacher's Notes

Estimate the length of your pencil. Write down your estimate. Now measure to check. Is your pencil longer or shorter than the pencil in the picture? Children will have pencils of different lengths so they could compare pencils to help visualize different lengths.

✔ Answers will vary.

➔ **Ask children to estimate the length of various classroom items, such as a piece of paper or a book, and then check their estimates with a ruler.**

2 Teacher's Notes

Jamil has a rectangle whose sides are three centimetres and four centimetres. Draw Jamil's rectangle. It can be in two orientations. Make sure children draw the sides at right angles to each other. Squared paper may be needed unless protractors are used for accuracy.

✔

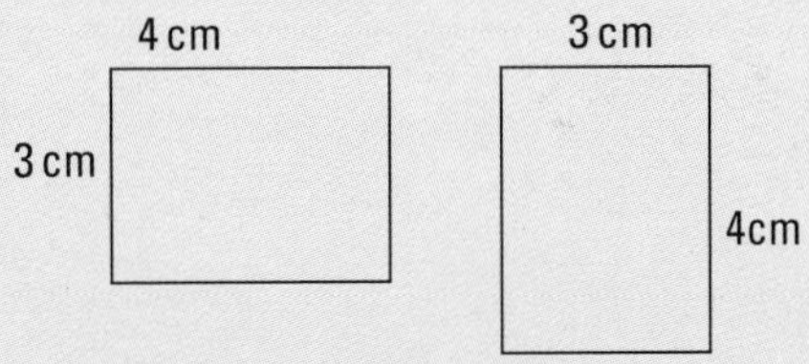

➔ ***Is it possible to draw another rectangle which also has sides of 3 cm and 4 cm, and which is different from the one you just drew?* (No, it will only be different in orientation.)**

3 Teacher's Notes

Estimate the length of this page in centimetres. Write your estimate, then measure to check. How close was your estimate? Children may estimate the length to be about 30 cm as this is the length of a large ruler which is very close to the actual value.

✔ 29.8 cm

➔ ***What is the width of the page?* (21 cm) *What is the length of the diagonal of the page?* (36·5 cm) *Estimate first, then measure.***

4 Teacher's Notes

With a partner, estimate the length of your own giant-sized step. Then help each other to measure them. How would you do this? Encourage children to explain their methods. A tape measure might be useful to have instead of rulers.

✔ The answers will vary depending on the child.

➔ ***If you took five of those giant-sized steps, what distance will you have covered?***

5 Teacher's Notes

Can you draw a rectangle with a perimeter of fourteen centimetres? Children will need to work out the possible dimensions of the rectangle(s) before they start drawing.

✔ These rectangles would all have perimeters of 14 cm: 1 cm and 6 cm, 2 cm and 5 cm or 3 cm and 4 cm.

➔ ***Look at all the possible rectangles. What do you notice about the total length of one long side and one short side?* (It is equal to half the perimeter.) *Can you explain why this is?***

💡 Support children with squared paper or a peg board and a piece of string 14 cm long, to help them find different possible rectangles.

Unit 5

Name ____________________

1 Ross is writing a capital letter that has at least 2 right angles. What could it be?

2 These dots are corners of a square.
Draw the square.

3 Here is a folded piece of paper with a bit cut out.
Draw what it will look like when it is unfolded.

4 Half of this shape is missing. What could the whole shape look like?

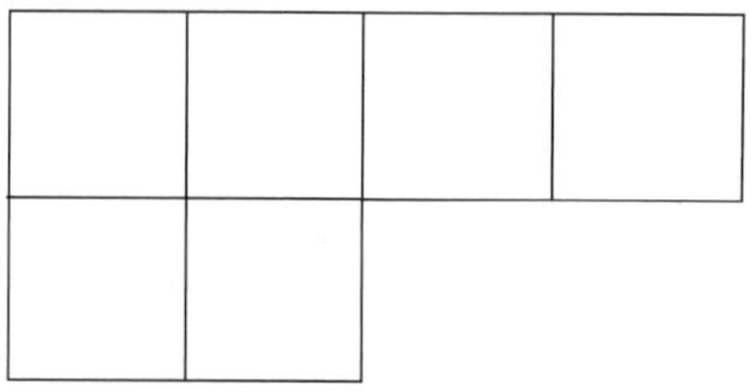

5 The number of lines of symmetry in this hexagon is the same as the number of sides. Is this true?

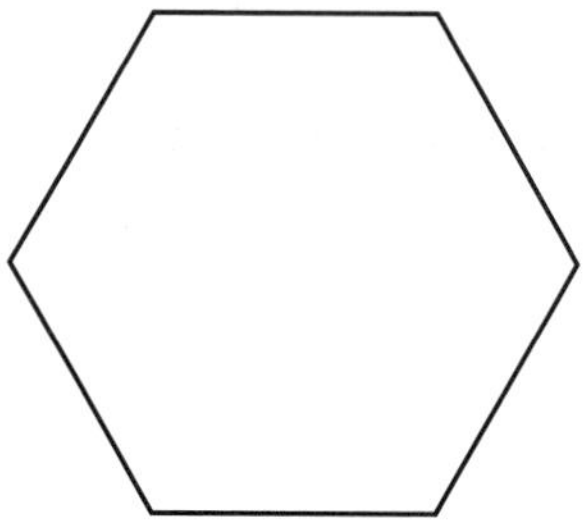

/5

Shape and space, reasoning about shapes

1 Teacher's Notes

Ross is writing a capital letter that has at least two right angles. What letter could it be? Encourage children to find more right angles in words, e.g. in their names written in capital letters.

✔ The letter could be E, F, H, or T.

➔ ***Which capital letters have the most right angles?*** **(E and H)**

2 Teacher's Notes

These two dots are two of the corners of a square. Draw the whole square. Make sure children measure the distance between the dots accurately, using a ruler.

✔ Check children have drawn a square with sides 3·5cm long.

➔ ***Is this shape a square?*** **(No, it is a rhombus.)**

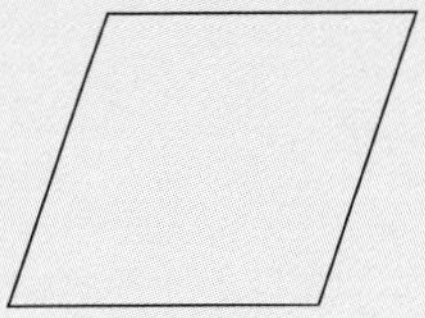

3 Teacher's Notes

Look at your worksheets. Here is a folded piece of paper with a small piece cut out as shown. Draw what the paper will look like when it has been unfolded. Ask children to try out the some with other shapes cut out of folded paper.

✔ A sheet of paper with a circle cut out in the middle.

➔ **In pairs, one child draws a shape on the fold of the paper and the other works out what the shape will look like when the paper is opened.**

4 Teacher's Notes

Half of this drawing of a shape is missing. What could the whole shape have looked like? In this question children have to remember that 'half' of the shape is missing so they have to add more than two squares to complete the shape.

✔

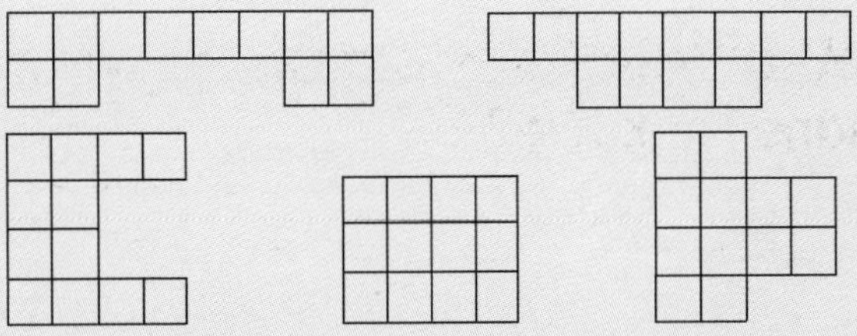

➔ ***Have you created all possible whole shapes? Compare your drawings with a partner's.***

5 Teacher's Notes

The number of lines of symmetry in a regular hexagon is equal to the number of sides. Do you think this is true or not? Show your answer with diagrams or by folding a paper hexagon.

✔ The statement is true.

➔ ***Is it true that the number of lines of symmetry in any regular polygon is equal to the number of sides?*** **(Yes)**

Unit 6

Name ______________________________

1 How many triangles can you find in this diagram?

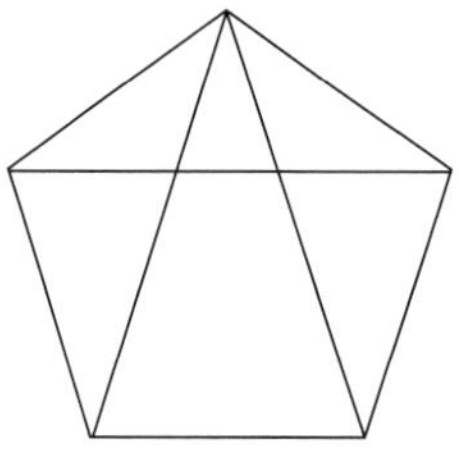

2 Roll 3 dice. Cut straws the same length in centimetres as the numbers you rolled. Try to make triangles with the straws.

3 Join dots to make some 2-d shapes. Label them if you know their names.

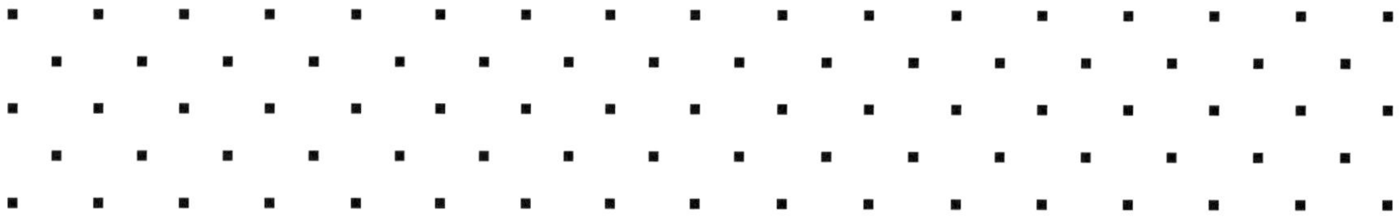

4 Which of these shapes are hexagons?

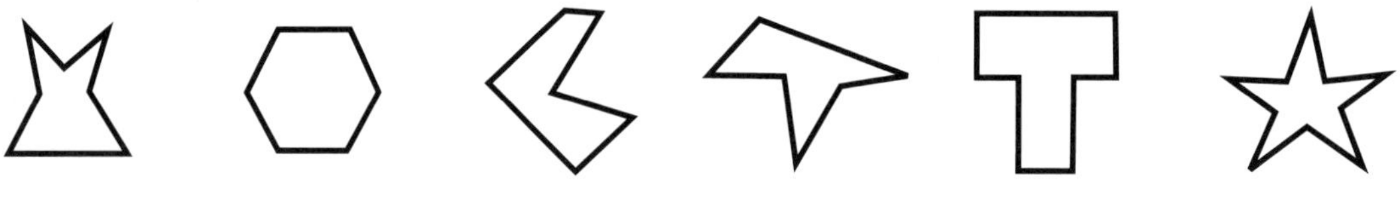

5 Here is an equilateral triangle. Investigate to find other shapes that you can make by joining 2, 3, or 4 of them together.

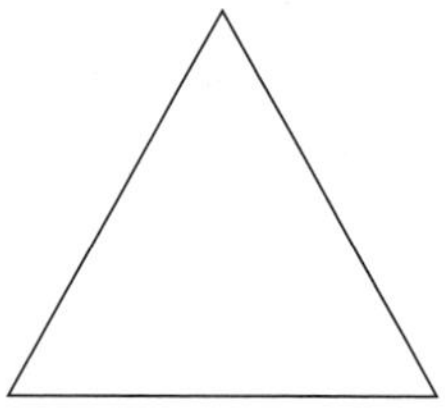

Shape and space, reasoning about shapes

1 Teacher's Notes

How many triangles can you find in the diagram on your worksheet? Look carefully. It may help children in counting the triangles to draw over them with coloured pencils.

11

Can you see any right angles? **(No)**

2 Teacher's Notes

Roll three dice and cut straws the same length in centimetres as the number you rolled. Try to construct a triangle with the straws. Some combinations of three numbers will make triangles, others won't. Make a list or table to show your findings. Scissors and straws are needed for this exercise.

There are lots of possible answers, because there are 56 different combinations of three numbers when rolling three 6-sided dice.

Is there a relationship between the length of the shorter sides and the longer sides, in the number combinations that do make triangles?

3 Teacher's Notes

Join the dots on this sheet to make different 2-d shapes. How many different shapes can you draw? Can you name them? Ask them to discuss the properties of each shape. They may need extra dotty paper to continue.

Lots of shapes are possible, including triangles, quadrilaterals and pentagons.

Do any of the shapes have lines of symmetry? If so, draw them on.

4 Teacher's Notes

What are the properties of a hexagon? Which of these shapes are hexagons? Ask children why the other shapes (non-hexagonal shapes) are not hexagons.

The second, third and fourth shapes are hexagons.

Draw another hexagon – try to make it as unusual as possible. Remember, you need six straight sides!

Ask children to name the other polygons and discuss their properties.

5 Teacher's Notes

Here is an equilateral triangle. Investigate to find the shapes that can be made by joining two, then three, and then four equilateral triangles together. Try to think of some good ways to do this. Coloured pencils might help children keep track of the sides of different triangles.

2 = rhombus. 3 = trapezium. 4 = large equilateral triangle. The children may not know the names of these shapes but can describe them.

Continue the investigation for five, six and seven equilateral triangles joined together.

You may choose to make tiles that the children can draw round again and again.

Unit 7

Name ______________________________

1 Circle the numbers that give an odd answer when added to 40.

32   3   12   45   65   341

2 Write the next number in this sequence.

101   97   93   89   85

3 What number would be in square 'A'?

119	122	125	128
131	134	137	140
143	146	A	152
155	158	161	164

4 Make as many even numbers as you can with these number cards. You can only use each card once each time.

1   2   7

5 Here is part of a calendar. How many patterns can you find?

JULY

MON	TUE	WED	THUR	FRI	SAT	SUN
		1	2	3	4	5
6	7	8	9	10	11	12
13	14	15	16	17	18	19
20	21	22	23	24	25	26

Properties of numbers and number sequences

1 Teacher's Notes

Which of these numbers give an odd number answer when you add them to 40? Circle the numbers that do. Encourage children to work out the answer mentally first.

3, 45, 65, 341.

If any odd number is added to forty, will the answer be odd or even? Can you explain how you know?

2 Teacher's Notes

Write down the next number in this sequence. Ask children to look for the 'pattern' in the sequence.

The pattern is '4 less' so the next number is 81.

Will the number fifty be included in the sequence? **(No)**

3 Teacher's Notes

What number would be in the square marked A? Children should try to see what number is added on each time to find the missing number in the sequence.

149

What patterns can you find in the grid of numbers? **(Each number is 3 more than the previous one. The numbers in each column go up 12 each time. Numbers in rows are alternately odd and even, but numbers in columns are either all odd or all even.)**

4 Teacher's Notes

On your worksheets are three number cards. Make as many even numbers as you can with them. You can use each card once or not at all each time. Children may need number cards to arrange to find all the possibilities.

2, 12, 72, 172, 712.

Ask children to do the same with these cards: 5, 2, 4.

Children should realise that to make different even numbers the necessary quality is that the 'units' digit is even.

5 Teacher's Notes

Here is part of a calendar. Find as many patterns as you can in ten minutes. A good start would be to ask children to choose a central number and then investigate its relation with the numbers around it.

There are many possible patterns. One is that any number is seven more than the one above it.

Look at two by two arrays of numbers in the calendar. Do you see any patterns in them? **(Each pair of opposite diagonal numbers adds to the same total.)**

Unit 8

Name ______________________

1 You can work out 3 x 4 by drawing 3 lines crossed by 4 lines and counting the crossing points. Show 3 x 5 this way. How are 3 x 4 and 3 x 5 related?

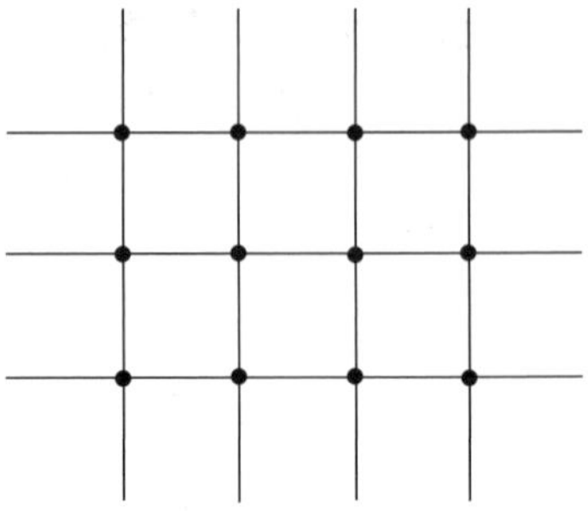

2 Answer these questions. What methods did you use?

a) Double 21

b) 6 x 15

c) 2 x 55

3 Does Aisha's method work?

4 Georgina has 2 numbers. If she adds them, she gets 11. If she multiplies them together she gets 30.

5 Gareth doubled these numbers. Which gave an even number answer?

143 **119**

123 **521**

Understanding multiplication and division

1 Teacher's Notes

You can find out what three times four is by drawing three lines crossed by four lines and then counting the crossing points. Draw lines to show three times five. Can you explain how three times four and three times five are related? Children will be able to use the given 3 x 4 grid to draw an extra column on, to make 3 x 5.

✔ 3 x 5 is 3 more than 3 x 4.

➔ **Ask children to think about the other facts that can be generated from the starting point of 3 x 5 = 15. Create a spider web to show them all:**

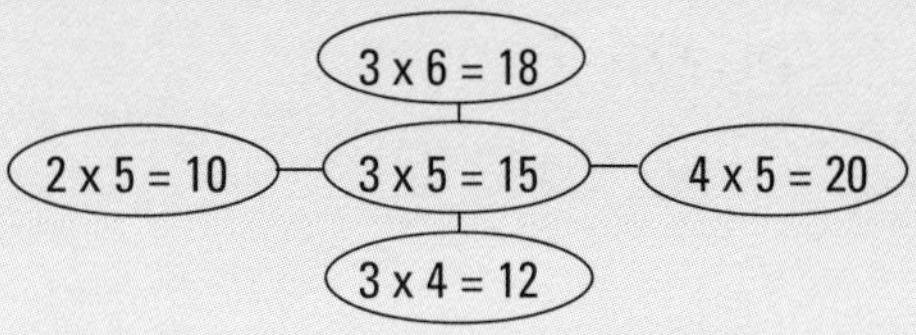

2 Teacher's Notes

Work with a partner. One of you reads out the question, and the other has ten seconds to calculate the answer. Change roles, then compare the strategies and jottings you have both used to reach the answer.

✔ a 42 b 90 c 110

➔ ***Can you use partitioning into hundreds, tens and ones to help you calculate five times one hundred and thirty-four?*** **(Yes, 5 x 100 = 500; 5 x 30 = 150; 5 x 4 = 20; answer = 670.)**

3 Teacher's Notes

Aisha has a method of multiplying by five. She multiplies a number by ten and then halves the result. Does Aisha's method work? Try out some examples to check your answer. Some children may be able to see why this method works. Ask them to think of other methods to multiply by 5.

✔ Yes, this method always works.

➔ ***Why does it always work?*** **(Because 10 is double 5, multiplying by 10 is the same as multiplying by 5 then 2.)**

4 Teacher's Notes

Georgina has two numbers. If she adds them she gets eleven. If she multiplies one by the other she gets thirty. What are her two numbers? This is a good reasoning question. Ask children to think of a similar question to ask their partner.

✔ The numbers are 6 and 5.

➔ ***I have two numbers. If I add them I get fourteen. If I multiply them I get forty-five. What are the numbers?*** **(5 and 9).**

5 Teacher's Notes

Gareth doubled each of the odd numbers on your worksheets. For each one, did he get an odd number or an even number answer? Work out the answers to check.

✔ For each one he got an even number.

➔ ***Why do you always get an even number when a whole number is doubled?*** **(When any number is doubled, it is multiplied by 2. All multiples of 2 are even numbers.)**

Unit 9

Name ______________________________

1 Mrs Andrews is planting bulbs.
She will plant 5 bulbs in each square.
How many will she plant?

2 Ruth and Beth found 12 eggs on an Easter egg hunt.
Beth found 2 more than Ruth. How many did they each find?

3 Make up a real life story for this number sentence.

4 x 90p = £3·60

4 How much would it cost for your family to go to this museum?

5 Farmer Bill has 75 sheep. Each sack of food costs £3·50 and feeds 15 sheep.
How many sacks does he need?
What does it cost?

—
5

Money and 'real life' problems, making decisions and checking results

1 Teacher's Notes

Mrs Andrews is planting some bulbs in her garden. She is going to plant five bulbs in each square. How many bulbs will she plant? Some children may wish to draw 5 dots in each square and then count the spots. Encourage them to try and do it mentally first.

45 bulbs.

Which of these number sentences fits the problem: 3 x 5, 3 x 3 x 5, or (3 x 3) + 5? **(3 x 3 x 5)**

2 Teacher's Notes

Ruth and Beth went hunting for Easter eggs. They found twelve eggs. Beth found two more eggs than Ruth. How many did they each find? A good starting point would be the case if they had collected equal numbers of eggs.

Ruth found 5 eggs and Beth found 7.

They decide to share their eggs with their friend Mary. How many eggs will each child get? **(4)**

3 Teacher's Notes

Make up a real life story to go with the number sentence on your worksheet. Make sure children remember to use the units (pounds and pence) of money while narrating their stories.

There are many possible answers, e.g. Jamie bought 4 ice-creams at 90p each and the total cost was £3·60.

Write the number sentence that goes with this real life story: Amanda bought a kite for £1·25 and a book for £2·30. She spent £3·55 altogether.

4 Teacher's Notes

Here are the entrance costs for a museum. How much would it cost for your family to go to this museum? Ask children to write down their calculations and check that they are correct.

This will depend on the members of children's families.

The museum has a special exhibition with Egyptian mummies on show. It costs an extra 50p per person to go inside. How much would it cost your family to go into the museum and into the special exhibition too?

5 Teacher's Notes

Farmer Bill has seventy-five sheep to feed. He buys sacks of sheep food for £3·50 per sack. Each sack will feed fifteen sheep. How many sacks should he buy and how much will it cost him? Children should write down all the information systematically as this will help them derive the answer.

75 ÷ 15 = 5 so he must buy five sacks of sheep food.
5 x £3·50 = £17·50. This is how much it will cost him.

If he doubles the number of sheep in his flock, how much will it cost him to feed them all? **(2 x £17·50 = £35)**

Unit 10

Name ____________________

1 Katie and Matthew made these biscuits.
They give one quarter to their dad.
Shade Dad's biscuits.

2 Describe the shaded part in 2 different ways.

3 Here is a geoboard cut into 2 matching shapes.
How else could you do this?

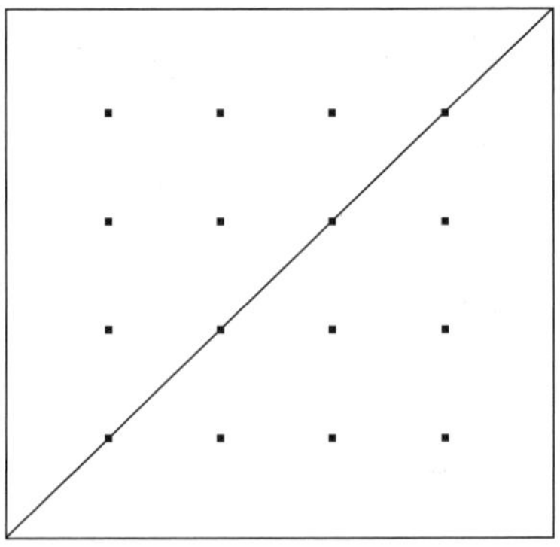

4 Circle $\frac{1}{3}$ of these balls.

5 Ahmed and Andrew each bought a pizza, and they ate half. Ahmed had more pizza left. Why?

5

Fractions and decimals

1 Teacher's Notes

Katie and Matthew made these biscuits. They want to give one quarter of the biscuits to their dad. Shade in Dad's biscuits. Before they start shading ask children what a 'quarter' is in fractions.

✔ Three biscuits should be shaded. They don't need to be next to each other.

➔ **Make up similar problems and challenge children to solve them visually, i.e. without calculating. There is no need to count the 12 biscuits in the original problem. The main point is to know that there are 6 in each row.**

2 Teacher's Notes

Look at your worksheets. Write, in two different ways, what the shaded part is. Remind children that we find fractions by looking at the number of equal parts a number or shape can be split into.

✔ $\frac{2}{8}$ or $\frac{1}{4}$

➔ **Ask children to show other fractions by shading more sections of the rectangle.**

3 Teacher's Notes

Ask children to look at their worksheets. *Here is a geoboard cut into two matching shapes. Show a different way of cutting the geoboard into two matching shapes. How many ways can you find?* Allow children to use squared paper to help them. Repeat with a 4 x 4 geoboard.

✔ Here is one possible answer:

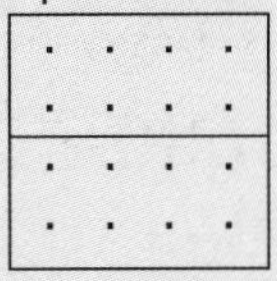

➔ ***Draw a rectangle on squared paper that is made up of twelve small squares. Find an unusual way to colour half of the rectangle.*** **(Work out the number of squares to colour in first by halving the number 12.)**

4 Teacher's Notes

Circle one third of these balls. Encourage children to draw one circle around the set of balls, rather than circling them individually. The visual split into three equal sets will be more obvious in this way.

✔ Children should circle 4 balls.

➔ ***How many balls would you circle if I asked for half of the balls?*** **(6)** ***Three quarters of the balls?*** **(9)** ***Two thirds of the balls?*** **(8)**

5 Teacher's Notes

Ahmed and Andrew each bought a pizza. Each ate half of his own pizza, but Ahmed had more pizza left than Andrew. How can this be? Ask children to use diagrams to demonstrate their answer.

✔ Ahmed's pizza was bigger to start with, so although they both ate 'half' they were different-sized halves.

➔ ***If the pizza were the same size and Ahmed eats three quarters of his and Andrew eats half of his, how much more pizza than Ahmed does Andrew have left?*** **($\frac{1}{4}$)**

Unit 11

Name ______________________________

1 Donal has 2 secret numbers – one is odd, one is even.
He adds the 2 numbers. Which of these is true?

- He gets an even number.
- He gets an odd number.
- You can't tell unless you know the numbers.

Odd + Even = ?

2 Consecutive numbers are ones that are next to each other in number order, like 3, 4 and 5.
Find 3 consecutive numbers that add up to 39.

3 John has 2 secret number cards.

The numbers add up to 15.
They multiply to give 54.

What are John's number cards?

4 Put the numbers 1 to 9 in the circles so that each row and column adds up to 15.

◯	◯	◯
◯	◯	◯
◯	◯	◯

5 I think of a number and subtract 18.
I get 26. What number did I start with?

/5

1 Teacher's Notes

Donal has two secret numbers, one of them is odd and one is even. He adds the two numbers. Which of the following is true? a) He gets an even number. b) He gets an odd number. c) There is no way to tell unless you know the secret numbers. Ask children to make up examples and investigate.

He gets an odd number.

Investigate what happens when you multiply an odd number with an even number.

2 Teacher's Notes

Consecutive numbers are those that are placed next to each other in number order. These are two sets of three consecutive numbers. Can you find a set of three consecutive numbers that add up to thirty-nine? Children should divide thirty-nine by three to get the middle number of the three.

12, 13, 14.

Which numbers between forty and fifty can be made by adding sets of three consecutive numbers?

Children should try and understand that a number needs to be divisible by three for there to be a set of three consecutive numbers adding up to make it.

3 Teacher's Notes

John has two mystery cards.
Clue 1: the numbers add to give fifteen
Clue 2: they also multiply to give fifty-four
This could be solved by elimination using both the clues. Alternatively, some children may know the six-times table which will be useful.

6 + 9 = 15
6 x 9 = 54
The mystery numbers are 6 and 9.

Make up a similar puzzle with two clues for a partner to solve.

4 Teacher's Notes

Arrange the numbers one to nine in these circles so that each row and column adds to give fifteen. Children should write in the first two or three numbers at random and then insert the others according to the conditions set.

One possible answer is:

6	2	7
1	9	5
8	4	3

Total numbers added together = 45. There are three rows, so each row must have a total of 15. Once the numbers in each row have been worked out, the positioning of them within each row depends on the numbers in each column – these must also total 15.

Is there more than one way to arrange the numbers?

5 Teacher's Notes

I think of a number then subtract eighteen. The answer is twenty-six. What number did I start with? Ask children to work this out mentally and then explain their method in writing.

26 + 18 = 44.

Choose a number. Add fifteen to your number. Subtract three. Now subtract twelve. What is your answer? Can you explain why this happened?

Unit 12

Name ____________________

1 How much money does each child have? Write them in order from most to least. One tally mark means 5p.

Name	Tally
Bradley	IIII
Emma	I
Meera	III
Megan	II
Ryan	~~IIII~~

2 In which classes are packed lunches more common than school dinners? How could you find out? Write down some ideas.

3 At what time of day do most vehicles drive in and out of the school car park? How could you find out? Write some suggestions.

4 In which game were most goals scored?

Did the Redhorns win?

Which game had the biggest goal difference?

Which game was a draw?

Which 2 games together had 8 goals?

Jackdaws	4	Sparrows	2
Greenbelts	0	Redhorns	3
Tigers	6	Lions	5
Truckers	1	Bikers	1

5 Put these numbers into the Venn diagram.

23 **41** **48** **72** **46** **16** **45** **11** **27** **35**

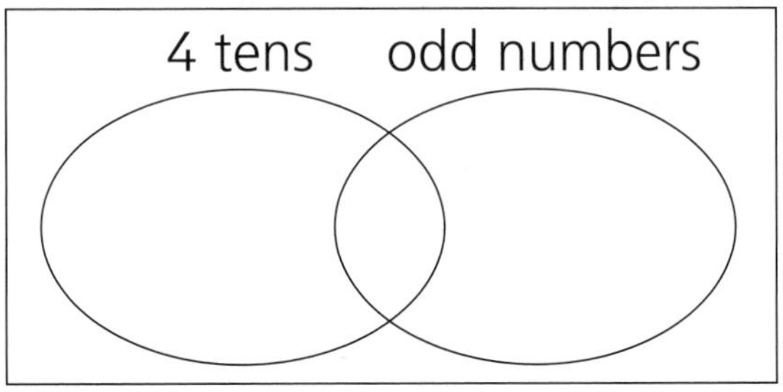

Handling data

1 Teacher's Notes

Here is a tally chart of the amount of money some children have in their pockets. Each tally represents 5p. List the children in order of the money they have from most to least. Work out how much money each child has.

Ryan: 25p, Bradley: 20p, Meera: 15p, Megan: 10p, Emma: 5p.

Ask children to create a tally chart like the one given so that the total amount of money that the children have is £3·70.

2 Teacher's Notes

In which classes in school are packed lunches more common than school dinners? What information do you need to gather to answer this question? What is the simplest way to gather this information? Where is this information held in school? How will you sort out the information?

Children should compile a chart or list with three columns showing class name, number of packed lunches, number of school dinners. The children may have gathered the information required from the dinner staff or teachers rather than asking individual children.

How many school dinners were served today? How many packed lunches? Can you give reasons for the difference in numbers?

3 Teacher's Notes

At what time of the day do most vehicles come into and go out of the school car park? Think carefully about how you could monitor this effectively without standing in the car park all day. Children should think about going into the car park at regular intervals and count the number of moving vehicles.

Methods will vary according to school circumstances. The most important thing is that discussions about effective collection of data should take place.

Present your findings visually in a bar chart or pictogram.

4 Teacher's Notes

On the worksheets are the results from the Sunday football league.
Use the chart to answer these questions:
a) In which game were most goals scored?
b) Did the Redhorns win or lose?
c) In which game was there the greatest goal difference?
d) Which game ended in a draw?
e) Which two games together involved a total of 8 goals?

a) Tigers v Lions.
b) The Redhorns won.
c) Greenbelts v Redhorns had the greatest goal difference of 3.
d) Truckers v Bikers ended in a draw.
e) Truckers v Bikers and Jackdaws v Sparrows had a total of 8 goals.

The next game involves the highest scoring team versus the lowest scoring team. Who will it be? **(Tigers v Greenbelts)**

5 Teacher's Notes

Place the following numbers into the Venn diagram. Children need to look at each number on the list individually and assess them against either criterion.

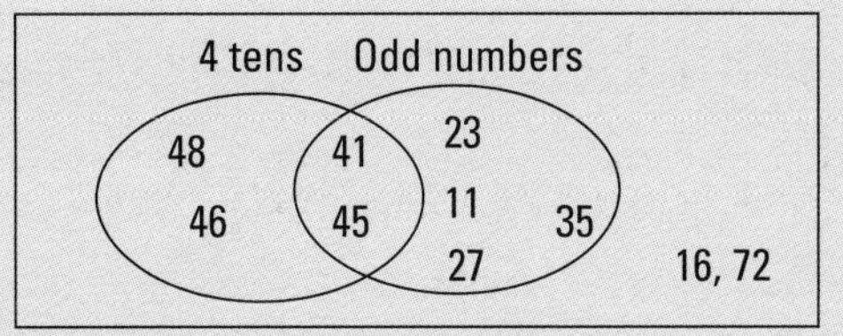

Which numbers cannot be placed and why? **(72, 16 - because they do not have 4 tens and they are not odd.)**

Unit 13

Name ____________________

1 Write 3 numbers that are smaller than –10.

2 How does the value of 5234 change if the '2' is changed to a '4'?

3 Instead of entering 6482 in her calculator, Jill entered 6492. By how much was she wrong?

4 Estimate the number the arrow is pointing to.

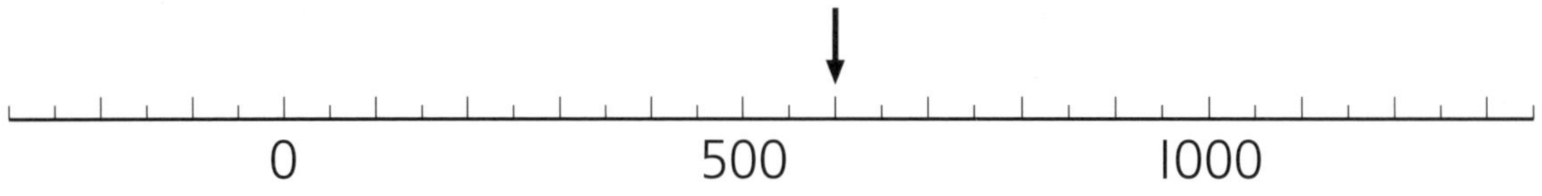

5 How can you change these numbers in one step?

3261	= 3561
6061	= 6461
1827	= 1867
8238	= 5238

5

Place-value, ordering, rounding and reading numbers from scales

1 Teacher's Notes

Write three numbers that are smaller than minus ten. Some children might like to draw a number line to help them.

There are many possible answers, for example –15, –25, –27.

Write three numbers between: four and nine; eight and minus three; minus one hundred and minus one hundred and fourteen.

The main thing for children to understand is that negative numbers decrease from right to left in a series symmetrical to the positive number series.

2 Teacher's Notes

How does the value of the number five thousand, two hundred and thirty four change if the two is changed to a four? Make sure children understand that the number increases by 200 exactly. Number cards could be used to check mental calculations.

The number is increased by 200.

What if the four in four thousand seven hundred and ninety-three were changed to a six?

3 Teacher's Notes

Instead of entering six thousand four hundred and eighty-two on her calculator, Jill entered six thousand four hundred and ninety-two. By how much was she wrong? Discuss with children how, by subtracting 10 on the calculator, Jill will be able to get back her original number.

10

***By how much would she have been wrong if she had entered seven thousand four hundred and eighty-two?* (1000)**

4 Teacher's Notes

What is a good estimate for the number the arrow is pointing to? Ensure that children understand that each division corresponds to 50 units, so the 12th division will be 600.

600

Show where these numbers are: three hundred, four hundred, two hundred and fifty. How did you decide where to put the numbers? Explain to your partner. Did they make the same decisions?

5 Teacher's Notes

How can you change the numbers in the first column to the numbers in the second column in one step? Ask children to write down their answers. Make sure they have the correct number of zeroes and '+' or '-' in each case.

+300, +400, +40, –3000.

***A secret number has been changed in the following ways: add two hundred, subtract thirty, add seven. It is now the number one thousand five hundred and thirty-nine. What was it to start with?* (1362)**

Unit 14

Name ____________________

1 How will you do this calculation?

32 + 28 =

Write some jottings to show how you did it.

2 Show how you can use a number line to find the difference between 17 and 50.

3 Is the sum of these numbers odd or even?

243 + 524 + 222 + 740 + 244

4 Choose three of these numbers to complete this number sentence.

1 **4** **3** **8**

☐☐ – ☐ = 38

5 Put the numbers 1–9 into the rings so each ring adds up to 15. Is there more than one way?

Understanding addition and subtraction

UNIT 14

1 Teacher's Notes

Ask children to look at their worksheets. *Here is a calculation. How would you do it? Write down some jottings to show how you did it.* The calculations by children should be clear and systematic.

There are a few methods. One method is: 32+28 = 32+30-2 = 62-2 = 60.

Samantha partitioned the 32 into 30 + 2 and the 28 into 20 + 8. She added the 'tens' numbers first to get 50, then the 'ones' numbers to get 10. Finally she added the 50 and 10 to get 60. Can you write out what she did? Can you complete the addition twenty-four plus fifty-three using Samantha's method?

2 Teacher's Notes

Can you show, or explain to a partner, how to use a number line to find the difference between seventeen and fifty? Children should explain how to move from 17 to 50 along the number line in stages, and then add all the increments to get the total difference.

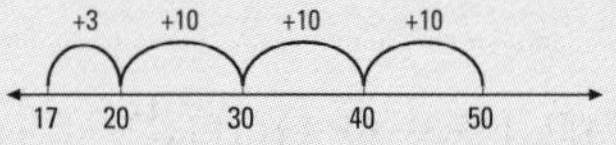

The difference between 17 and 50 is 33 because you need to count on another 33 to get from 17 to 50.

Complete this jotting to calculate the difference between thirty-six and one hundred and twenty.

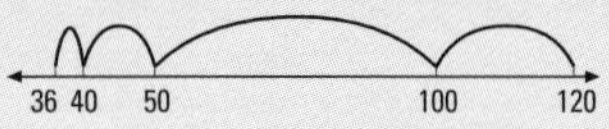

(+ 4, + 10, + 50, + 20 = difference of 84)

3 Teacher's Notes

Is the sum of these numbers odd or even? Can you tell without adding them? Some children may realise that if the number of odd numbers is odd, the addition will give an odd number.

The answer will be odd – we can tell it will be odd because if the number of odd numbers to be added is odd, whatever the number of even numbers, the addition will always equal an odd answer.

Show how you can add the numbers together to check. Which method will you use? Can you do it mentally or would jottings help? Will you need to use a written method of some kind?

4 Teacher's Notes

Choose three numbers from the set on the worksheet to make the number sentence true. Allow children to try out different combinations of numbers mentally before they write anything down.

41 – 3 = 38

What other number sentences can you make that use the numbers one, three, four, eight and the plus, minus and equals signs?

5 Teacher's Notes

Place the numbers one to nine inside these three rings so that the total inside each ring is 15. How many different ways can you find to do it? Are there any patterns that can be used? For this question children could choose one number between one to nine as a starting point and then work out what the other two would be to get a total of fifteen.

One way is: (6, 2, 7), (1, 9, 5), (8, 4, 3).

***If we used the numbers eleven to nineteen, what would the total inside each ring need to be for the puzzle to work?* (The sum of 11 to 19 divided by 3 = 45)**

Unit 15

Name ____________________

1 Marcus bought some crisps with a £1 coin.
The shopkeeper said "22, 23, 24, 25, 30, 50, £1."
What was the shopkeeper doing?

2 Vowels are worth 15p and consonants 10p.
Who in your family has the most expensive name?

3 The children on a camping trip will need tents.
Each tent holds 6 children, and has either girls or boys. There are 28 girls and 37 boys.
How many tents will be needed?

4 Mandy bought 3 tins of paint at £4·73 each.
What change did she get from £20?

5 One game at the fair costs 20p. Emily has £5.
How many games can she play?

Money and 'real life' problems, making decisions and checking results

UNIT 15

1 Teacher's Notes

Marcus bought some crisps for 21p. He gave the shopkeeper a one pound coin. The shopkeeper said, 'Twenty-two, twenty-three, twenty-four, twenty-five, thirty, fifty, one pound'. Explain what the shopkeeper was doing. Ask children what the change will be in coins.

The shopkeeper is counting up in available coins to find the difference between the price of the crisps and the money given by Marcus. This will tell him the change to give: four 1p coins, one 5p coin, one 20p coin and one 50p coin.

Use the shopkeeper's method to work out the change from £1 when 43p is spent.

2 Teacher's Notes

Vowels are worth 15p and consonants are worth 10p. Who in your family has the most expensive name? Ask children to work out the worth of each name and check their answers.

Answers will vary.

Is the longest name always the most valuable? **(No, it depends on the proportions of vowels and consonants in each name.)**

3 Teacher's Notes

Some children are going on a camping trip and they will be sleeping in tents. Each tent holds six children, and each tent has either boys or girls. There are twenty-eight girls and thirty-seven boys going on the trip. How many tents will be needed? Check the calculations of the children.

Girls' tents: 28 ÷ 6 = 4 r4 so 5 tents needed.
Boys' tents: 37 ÷ 6 = 6 r1 so 7 tents needed.
Total tents needed = 12.

Each tent costs £45 to buy. How much will it cost to buy 12 new tents? **(£450 + £90 = £540)**

4 Teacher's Notes

Mandy bought three tins of paint at £4·73 each. What was her change from £20? Encourage children to do calculations clearly in a way that is self-explanatory – as it is in the Answer.

Total cost 3 x £4·73 = £14·19.
Change = £20·00 – £14·19 = £5·81.

Each tin of paint was reduced in the sale by £1·50. How much do the three tins cost her now? **(£9·69)**

Ask children to say their answer out in words stating how many pounds and pence there are in change.

5 Teacher's Notes

One game at the fair costs 20p. How many games can Emily play with her £5? Tell children to break up the question into manageable parts.

There are five 20p's in each pound so there are twenty-five 20p's in £5. Emily can play 25 games at the fair.

How many games priced at 40p could she play with the same amount of money? **(12 goes and 20p left over)**

Unit 16

Name ______________________________

1 How heavy are the whole lot of tomatoes in kilograms?

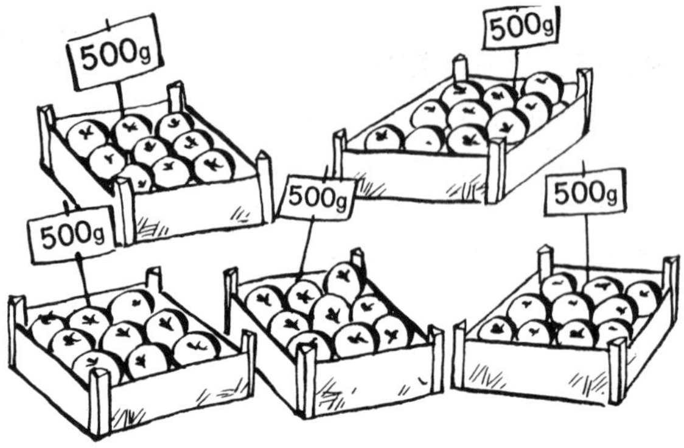

2 The cook needs 100g of potatoes for each portion of chips. How many kilograms of potatoes does the cook need to feed everyone in your class?

3 Put these in order from smallest to largest.

gram kilogram half-kilogram

Where would a milligram come in this order?

4 Jane's mother has a list of ingredients to make biscuits for 6 people. What would she need for 3 people? 12 people?

5 Work in pairs. Estimate the time needed to write all the odd numbers from 1 to 50.

Time each other as you write them out. How close were you?

Measures, including problems

1 Teacher's Notes

How heavy are the whole lot of tomatoes in kilograms? Children should observe the artwork and then use the information given to find the answers.

$2\frac{1}{2}$ kg.

Let children collect items such as books, building blocks and so on, which add up to about $2\frac{1}{2}$ kg. They should check the weight on balance scales.

2 Teacher's Notes

The school cook wants to buy potatoes to make one portion of chips for each child in your class. One hundred grams of potatoes are needed for each portion. About how many kilograms of potatoes should he buy? Some answers may be in decimal numbers.

The answer depends on the number of children in the class and will be the number of children multiplied by 100 g. The answer should be given in kilograms and grams.

How many kilograms of potatoes would be needed to give everyone in your family a portion of chips?

3 Teacher's Notes

Put the amounts in order from smallest to largest. Where do you think a milligram would come in that order? Ask children to write the correct order down. Make sure they know the abbreviations too: mg, g, $\frac{1}{2}$ kg, kg.

Milligram, gram, half-kilogram, kilogram.

Find three items in the food cupboard whose total weight is about one kilogram.

Ask children to notice the prefixes milli-, centi-, etc., and discuss what other measures use these.

4 Teacher's Notes

Jane's mother has a list of the ingredients needed to make biscuits for six people. Imagine that she wanted enough biscuits for three people or for twelve people. How would she need to alter the ingredients list? The rules will apply to the whole list so there is no need to see the actual list of ingredients.

For three people halve all the ingredients; for twelve people double all the ingredients.

What would Jane's mother do if she wanted to make biscuits for just one person?

5 Teacher's Notes

Work with a partner. Estimate how long it would take to write down all the odd numbers from one to fifty. Now use a stopwatch to time each other as you complete the task. How close were your estimates?

Answers will vary.

Think of a task that would take a shorter amount of time to do. Set each other the challenge of beating your own time with the new task set.

Unit 17

Name ____________________

1 My square has sides that are a whole number of centimetres long. Which of these can be the perimeter of my square? Why?

8 cm **15 cm**

90 cm **57 cm**

2 Put these shapes in order by area, from smallest to largest.

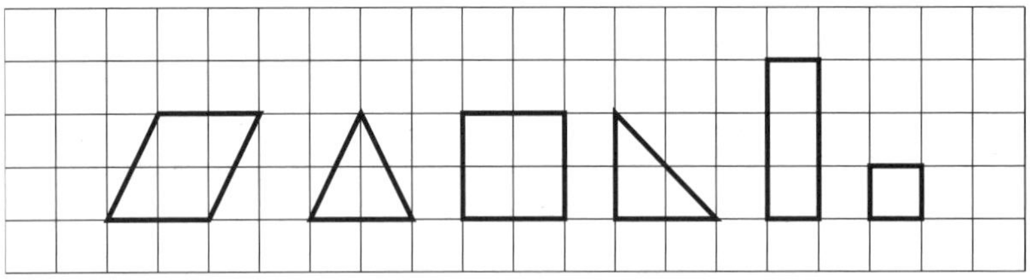

3 This square has an area of 9 square units. Draw another shape with the same area.

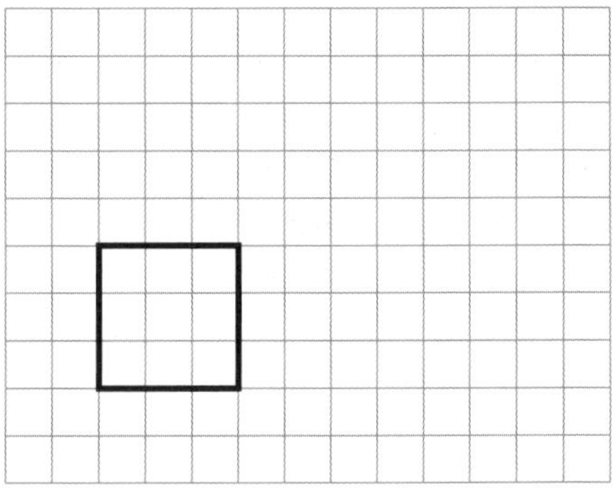

4 Here is a small geoboard. Draw 2 shapes with perimeters of 10 cm.

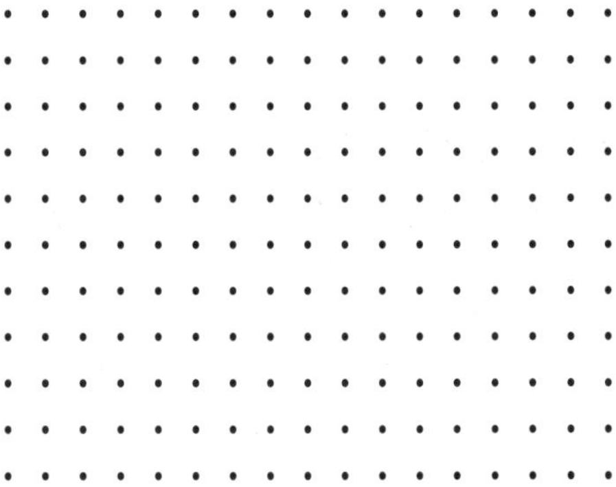

5 Each square means a 1 m by 1 m square of garden. Plan 2 gardens with an area of 4 square metres. Are they rectangles?

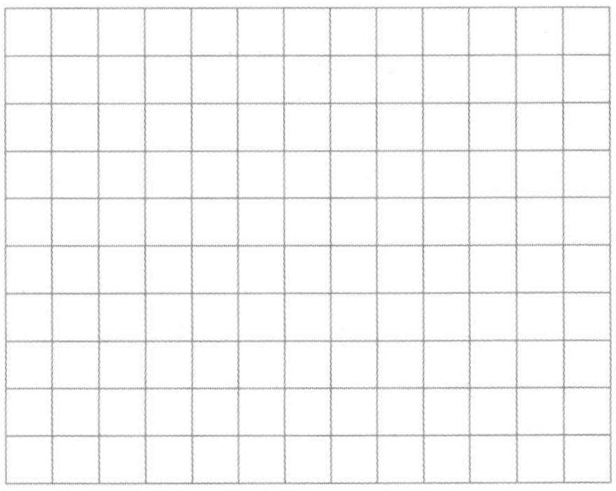

Measures – area and perimeter

1 Teacher's Notes

Imagine a square. The sides are all a whole number of centimetres. Which of these lengths is a possible perimeter of the square? The perimeter of a square is four times the length of a side.

8 cm (The perimeter must be a multiple of 4.)

How did you decide on your answer? What is the perimeter of a square with sides five centimetres long?

2 Teacher's Notes

Put these shapes in order by their area, from smallest to largest. Children should count the number of squares occupied by each shape. Some shapes may occupy an area that includes half-squares, like rhombuses. Triangles may be viewed as half a rectangle divided along the diagonal. The area will be half of the rectangle.

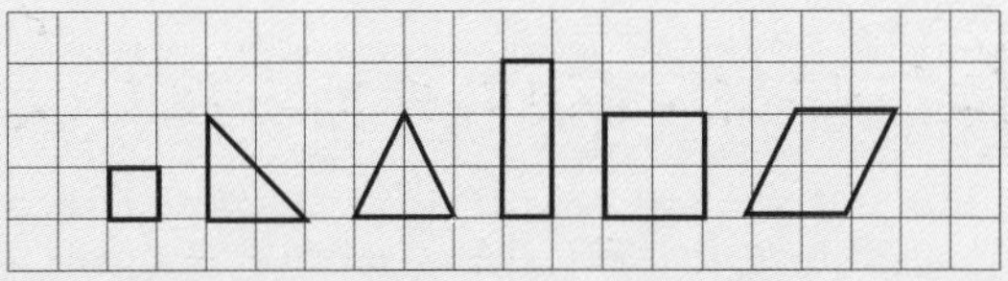

Area (sq units) 1 2 2 3 4 4

Using centimetre-squared paper, draw rectangles whose area are ten square centimetres. How many different rectangles can you draw?

3 Teacher's Notes

Here is a square with an area of nine square units. Draw a different shape (not a square) which has the same area.

There are many possible answers, the simplest is a rhombus of sides 3 units.

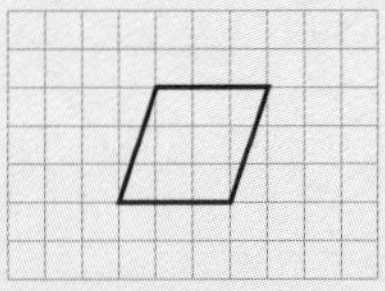

***Can you draw a triangle which has an area of nine square centimetres?* (The best way to do this is to draw a rectangle with an area of 18 square centimetres and divide it in half.)**

4 Teacher's Notes

Here is a small geoboard. Draw two different shapes that have perimeters of ten centimetres. Make sure children think about making different shapes: squares, rectangles, triangles.

There are many possible answers, for example: rectangle of sides 2 cm and 3 cm, or triangle of sides 2 cm, 3 cm, 5 cm.

***Draw a rectangle with an area of four square centimetres and a perimeter of ten centimetres?* (The rectangle is 1cm x 4 cm.)**

5 Teacher's Notes

Each square on this grid represents a gardener's drawing of a one metre by one metre square area. Plan out two different gardens, each of which is four square metres in area. Are either of them rectangular in shape? Check the shapes children draw.

Possible gardens with areas of 4 square metres would be 1 m x 4 m and 2 m x 2 m. They are both rectangles. A square is a special kind of rectangle where the sides are of equal lengths.

***Are any other answers possible?* (Rhombus with sides 2 m x 2 m.)**

Unit 18

Name ____________________

1 This is a box that has been cut and flattened.
The shaded square is the top of the box.
Shade the bottom of the box.

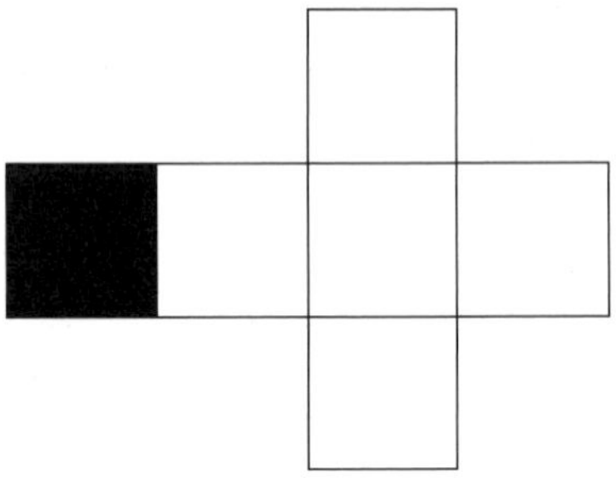

2 Estimate the size of this angle.

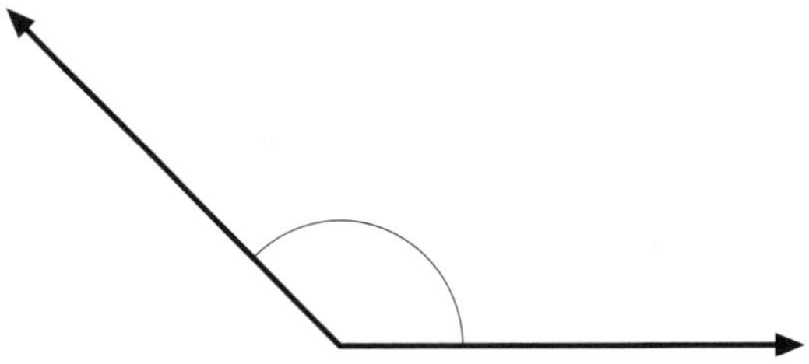

3 How many cubes do you need to make this block?

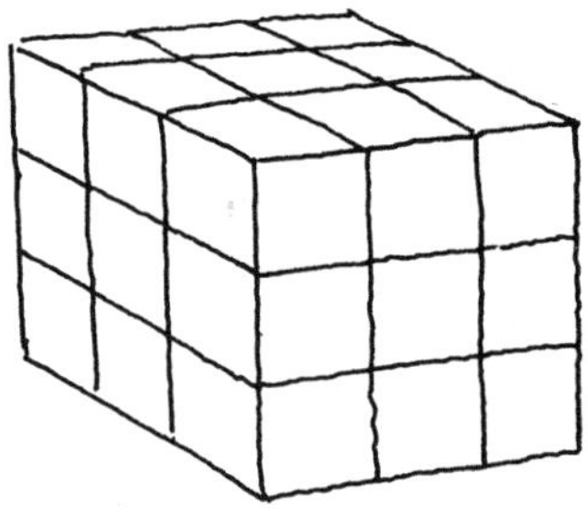

4 This triangular pyramid was painted red and put on a table. Draw the paint mark it would make.

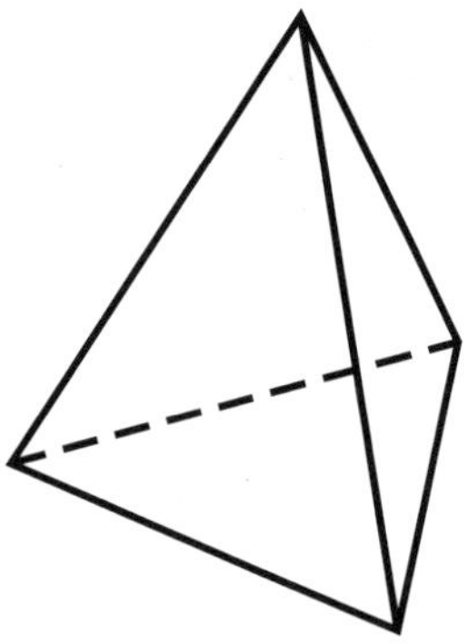

5 Is this true? All pyramids have an even number of edges. Investigate to find out.

5

Shape and space, reasoning about shapes

UNIT 18

1 Teacher's Notes

This diagram shows the faces of a box after it has been cut and flattened. We call this the 'net' of the box. The shaded square is the top of the box. Shade in the bottom of the box. Check the answer to see that the correct square has been shaded.

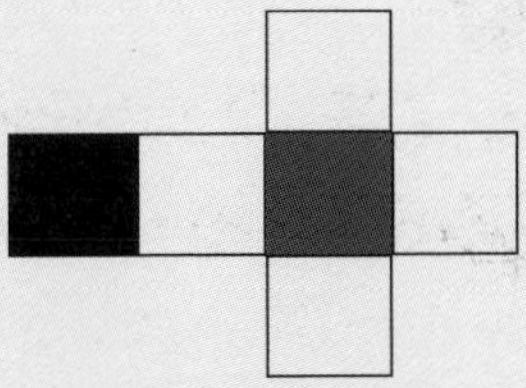

Could the box have been cut in different places creating a different 'net'?

2 Teacher's Notes

Estimate the size of this angle. Use your knowledge about the size of right angles to help you estimate. The angle is greater than 90° and halfway between 90° and 180°. It is one and a half right angles. Allow children to verify their estimates by using a protractor.

135°

What is the sum of the angles in a rectangle? Remember to use your knowledge about the size of right angles to help you. **(360°)**

3 Teacher's Notes

How many cubes are needed to make this block? One method is to imagine the block as made up of 3 layers of 3 x 3 squares placed one behind the other to make a (3 x 3) x 3 block. Build the block using cubes to confirm answers.

27

In the first question the block was three by three by three cubes. How many cubes are needed to make a four by four by four block?

4 Teacher's Notes

Imagine that this triangular pyramid is painted red all over and placed on a table. Draw the paint mark that the shape would leave on the table. Children could look at 3-d shapes to help them visualise the answer.

A triangle of the same size and orientation as the base of the pyramid.

What paint marks might be left by a cone? **(A circle)**

5 Teacher's Notes

Investigate to find out whether this statement is true or not. All pyramids have an even number of edges. Encourage children to draw and look at the bases, e.g. triangular, square, hexagonal.

This is true.

Can you explain why this is true? **(This is true because pyramids are formed by extending edges from each corner of the base shape to the apex. The number of edges on any pyramid is therefore double the number of edges on the base, i.e. even. Triangle base = 6 edges, square base = 8 edges, pentagon base = 10 edges, etc.)**

Unit 19

Name ____________________

1 Count on in 4s from 902. Don't go past 930.
How many numbers will you say? Can you work it out without counting?

2 If this pattern continues, what will B be if A=20?

A	B
4	24
8	48
12	72
9	54

3 Nilima counts back from 9 in 2s. Continue the counting for 4 more steps. Can you see any patterns?

9 7 5 3 1 –1

4 Every third bead is black. How many black beads are there between 1 and 40?

5 Start at –1. Count backwards in threes.
Will you say –30? Why?

/5

Properties of numbers, number sequences and reasoning about numbers

1 Teacher's Notes

Count on in fours from nine hundred and two. Do not go past nine hundred and thirty. How many numbers do you think you will say? How can you calculate it without counting? The last part of the question requires reasoning and children should be encouraged to explain how they got the answers.

✔ 902, 906, 910, 914, 918, 922, 926. There will be 7 numbers. 930 – 902 = 28 and 28 ÷ 4 = 7.

➔ ***Do you see any pattern in the numbers?***

2 Teacher's Notes

If the pattern in the table continues, what will B be if A is 20? Ask children to explain this reasoning.

✔ B is 120. (It is the six times table.)

➔ ***If B is three hundred and sixty six, what is A?*** **(61)**

3 Teacher's Notes

Nilima counts back from nine in twos. Continue the counting for four more steps. Can you describe any patterns that you see? Children should see the symmetry in the number sequence they generate.

✔ 9, 7, 5, 3, 1, –1, – 3, –5, –7, –9. The positive and negative numbers in the series are symmetrical across zero.

➔ ***Start at six and count back in fours. Will a symmetrical number pattern appear as it did in the previous example? Can you explain how this pattern is different?***

💡 Using a number line is a good way to establish how negative numbers work.

4 Teacher's Notes

Every third bead on the string is black. How many black beads are there between one and forty? Children need to count on in threes till they get to thirty-nine.

✔ 13

➔ ***How many black beads are there between one and one hundred?*** **(33)**

💡 Encourage children to think of a way to estimate the answer without counting on. This is done by dividing the final number by the increment value (3) – the quotient is the answer.

5 Teacher's Notes

If you count backwards from negative one in threes will negative thirty be on the list? Can you explain why? Children should observe the number pattern generated to predict the answer.

✔ No

➔ ***Will negative one hundred be on the list?*** **(Yes). It may help children to see the number pattern if you shade numbers said on a hundred square, imagining that they are negative numbers.**

Unit 20

Name ____________________

1 Can a number be a multiple of 4, and not a multiple of 2? Explain your answer.

2 Is Ingrid right? Use examples to explain your answer.

> When you double a 2-digit number, the answer is always a 2-digit number.

3 Philip wrote the numbers from 1 to 200. How many multiples of 5 did he write?

4 This is how Stephen worked out 23 x 4. Explain what he did.

	20	3	
4	80	12	= 92

5 Double 49. Write instructions telling someone else how to do it.

1 Teacher's Notes

Is it possible for a number to be a multiple of four and not a multiple of two? Explain your answer. Encourage children to explain their reasoning clearly and not just by stating examples.

No, every multiple of 4 is also a multiple of 2. Answers in the 4 times table are double answers in the 2 times table.

Does it work the other way round? Is every multiple of two a multiple of four? **(No)**

2 Teacher's Notes

Ingrid says that when you double a 2-digit number the answer is always a 2-digit number, e.g. twenty-three doubled gives forty-six. Is she right? Can you list some examples that show whether this is true or not?

Ingrid is wrong. Doubles of 2-digit numbers from 10 to 49 give a 2-digit answer, but numbers larger than 49, when doubled, give a 3-digit answer.

Write a statement onto a piece of paper and pass to a partner. They have to work out whether the statement is true or not.

3 Teacher's Notes

Philip wrote the numbers from one to two hundred. How many multiples of five did he write? Ask children to be systematic in their approach. They could break up the question into more manageable parts.

40. Starting with 5 every fifth number up to 200 is a multiple of 5. Number of multiples is thus 200 divided by 5.

How many multiples of two did Philip write? **(100)**

4 Teacher's Notes

This is how Stephen worked out twenty-three times four. Explain in writing what Stephen did, using jottings and notes. You might want to complete another multiplication like this to check that your explanation works!

Stephen partitioned 23 into 20 + 3. He multiplied 20 by 4 to get an answer of 80. Then he multiplied 3 by 4 to get an answer of 12. Finally he added 80 and 12 together to get his answer of 92.

Use Stephen's method to calculate forty-eight times six and thirty-four times six.

5 Teacher's Notes

Double forty-nine. Then write instructions to tell someone else how to double forty-nine. Encourage children to think of different ways of approaching the problem.

One way is to double 50 and subtract two. Another is to partition 49 into 40 + 9, double 40, double 9 and add the two answers together.

Double forty-eight. Then write out instructions for someone to follow.

Unit 21

Name ____________________

1 Olivia has £10·35 in 5p coins. How many coins does she have?

2 Rhys puts 8 stamps on each page of his album. How many pages does he need for 50 stamps?

3 How many 10p coins are needed to make £12·30?

4 Make up a real life story to show 49 ÷ 4 = 12 remainder 1.

5 John wants to buy the book. He saves 30p each week How long will it be before he can buy it?

5

Money and 'real life' problems, making decisions and checking results

UNIT 21

1 Teacher's Notes

Olivia has £10·35 in 5p coins. How many coins does she have? Children could start by estimating how many 5p coins there are in £10.

207. Ask children to explain how they reached their answer. An important tactic of problem solving is to break a problem into manageable parts. Accordingly, £10 gives 100 ten pence coins and therefore 200 five pence coins; £0·35 gives seven more 5p coins.

How can £10·35 be made using the fewest notes and coins? **(£10 note, 20p, 10p, 5p)**

2 Teacher's Notes

Rhys is a stamp collector. He puts eight stamps on each page in his album. How many pages will he need for fifty stamps? Check that children understand how to approach the problem. Some children may know the eight times table while others will divide fifty by eight to get the answer.

He will need 7 pages. The last page will have only two stamps.

How many pages will be needed for one hundred stamps?

3 Teacher's Notes

How many 10p coins are needed to make £12·30? One method would be to convert the amount into pence and then divide it by ten.

123

How many 5p coins make £12·30? **(246)**

4 Teacher's Notes

Make up a real life story to show that forty-nine divided by four equals twelve remainder one. Ask children to speak out their stories aloud. Encourage children to try out varied possibilities for their stories.

One possible story is 'Sean had 49 marbles. He gave them out equally to four friends. How many marbles were left over?'

What is different if there are fifty marbles? **(The remainder is 2.)**

5 Teacher's Notes

John wants to buy a book that costs £4·50. He saves 30p each week. How many weeks must he save for before he can afford to buy the book? Encourage children to break up the problem into parts if they struggle with the question.

15 weeks.

Approximately how many months is this? **(It is between 3 and 4 months.)**

Unit 22

Name ____________________

1 George spent $\frac{1}{4}$ of his savings on a CD. How much was the CD if his savings were £24?

2 This bottle holds 2 litres of lemonade. Each cup can hold $\frac{1}{4}$ of a litre. How many cups can Amy fill?

3 Is this true? Halfway between any 2 multiples of 10 there is a multiple of 5.

4 What fraction of this shape is shaded?

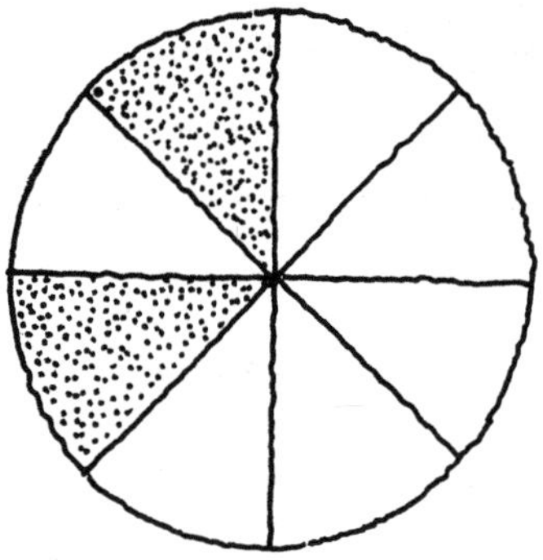

5 What has been added to these numbers?

4·6 ⟶ 4·9
3·2 ⟶ 3·5
2·1 ⟶ 2·4
17·9 ⟶ 18·2

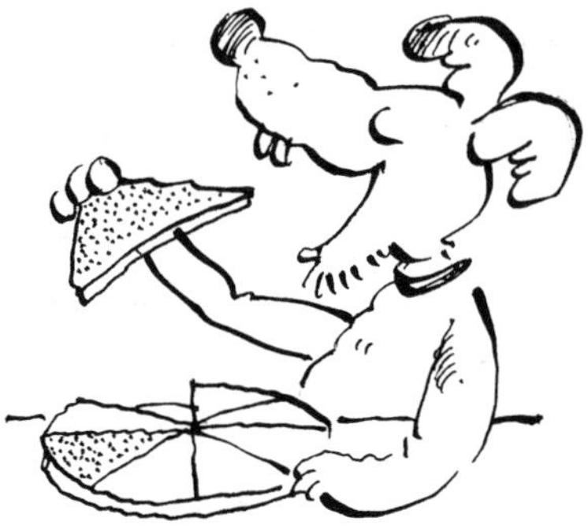

Fractions and decimals

1 Teacher's Notes

George spent a quarter of his savings on a CD. How much did the CD cost if his savings were originally £24? Children should be clear about the question. They need to calculate a quarter of 24 and write it in pounds.

£6

George spent half of the money that was left on a football shirt. How much in savings did he have at the end? **(£9)**

Ask children to explain the sequence of events that happened, starting with £24.

2 Teacher's Notes

The bottle of lemonade holds two litres. Amy is filling plastic cups with the lemonade. If each cup holds quarter of a litre, how many will she be able to fill? Ask children to be systematic in their calculations.

8 cups.

If she used smaller cups which only held one sixth of a litre, how many cups could she fill? **(12)**

3 Teacher's Notes

Is this statement true? Halfway between any two multiples of ten there is amultiple of five. Try out different numbers to see whether this is true or not. Remind children that all multiples of ten are also multiples of five.

True, for example : 70 ---------105 ----------140.

Ask children to investigate whether the same thing happens with multiples of 3 halfway between two multiples of 6.

4 Teacher's Notes

What fraction of this shape is shaded? Some children may need help grasping that the 2 shaded triangles may not be adjacent to one another. They just have to count the shaded triangles which are worth $\frac{1}{8}$ each.

$\frac{2}{8}$ or $\frac{1}{4}$

Explore with the children the number relationship between the numerators and denominators of $\frac{1}{4}$ and $\frac{2}{8}$. Can they use this pattern to devise other fractions equivalent to $\frac{1}{4}$ and $\frac{2}{8}$? ($\frac{3}{12}$, $\frac{4}{16}$, $\frac{5}{20}$ ...)

5 Teacher's Notes

What has been added to each of these numbers? If children need prompting tell them to count in decimal numbers from the start number and stop when they get to the finish number.

0·3 has been added.

Count from zero in steps of zero point three, writing down each number that you say. Can you see a pattern? Describe it. **(0·3, 0·6, 0·9, 1·2, 1·5, 1·8... similar to 3 times table pattern)**

Unit 23

Name ______________________

1 How many of each animal are there?

$\frac{1}{2}$ the animals are dogs

$\frac{1}{4}$ are cats

10 of the animals are cats

2 are reptiles

$\frac{1}{5}$ are birds

2 The DIY shop has wood in these lengths. Hannah needs 8·75 m of wood. How many ways can she do this?

WOOD STRIPS

75 cm
1 m
150 cm
2·75 m
300 cm
4·5 m
6 m

3 Round these amounts to the nearest pound.
Which whole pound amount is most common?

£15·32	£15·67	£15·37
£14·89	£13·48	£15·72
£13·78	£14·35	£13·56
£13·96	£15·51	£14·20
£14·23	£13·21	£15·80

4 Place these decimals on the number line: **1·7 0·4 1·3 0·7 1·2 0·2**

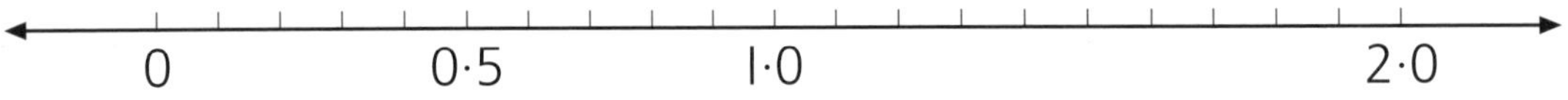

5 Shade $\frac{1}{3}$ of this shape. How many ways can you do it?

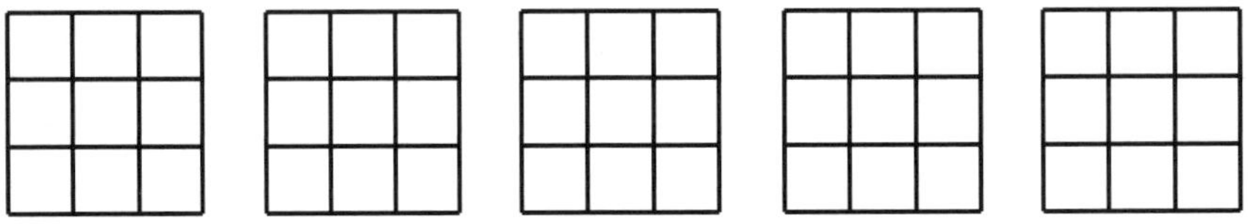

Fractions and decimals

1 Teacher's Notes

There are lots of animals in the rescue centre. Can you work out how many of each animal type there are from the clues? Ask children to read the question carefully. The clue has to do with cats.

20 dogs, 10 cats, 8 birds, 2 reptiles.

Make up a similar fraction problem for a partner to solve. Make sure you give them enough information to make the puzzle possible!

2 Teacher's Notes

The DIY shop has strips of wood in various lengths. Hannah needs to buy enough wood to make a total length of eight and three-quarter metres. How many different ways can she do this? Ask children to write down three different answers.

Various answers possible including: 6 m + 2·75 m, 300 cm + 300 cm + 2·75 m, 4·5 m + 150 cm + 2·75 m...

Hannah wants to make as few joins in the pieces of wood as possible. Which lengths should she buy?

3 Teacher's Notes

If each of these amounts were rounded to the nearest pound, which whole pound amount would be most common? Ask children to make a table showing the rounded whole number corresponding to each of the amounts in the worksheet.

Rounded to £13 = £13·48, £13·21.
Rounded to £14 = £13·78, £13·96, £14·23, £14·35, £13·56, £14·20.
Rounded to £15 = £15·32, £14·89, £15·37.
Rounded to £16 = £15·51, £15·67, £15·72, £15·80.
The most common whole pound answer is £14.

Why did £13 have the fewest amounts rounded to it?

4 Teacher's Notes

Place these decimals on the number line. Tell children to mark and label their points clearly on the number line. Might be useful to have coloured pencils.

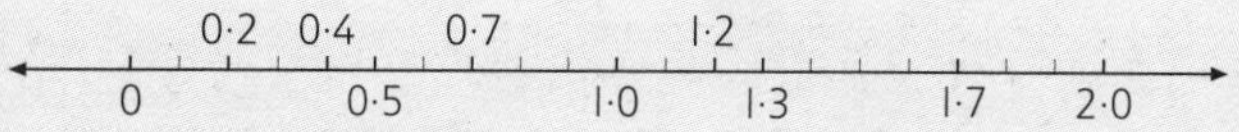

Use the number line to calculate the following:
1·3 + 0·6
1·8 – 1·3
0·4 + 1·3
1·6 – 0·9

5 Teacher's Notes

How many different ways can you shade one third of this shape? Once they complete the task ask children to see how the others have done theirs so that they look at different possible ways to demonstrate one third.

There are many possible answers, as long as each time 3 of the 9 equal parts (or equivalent to 3, i.e. 6 halves of the 9 whole equal parts) are shaded each time. The important thing for children to realise is that the 3 parts do not have to be placed together for it to still show $\frac{1}{3}$ of the shape shaded.

***How many equal parts need to be shaded to show two thirds shaded?* (6)**

Unit 24

Name ______________________________

1 What sort of sport do children in your class play? How would you gather this information? Present your findings in a table.

2 Sort these shapes into the Venn diagram.

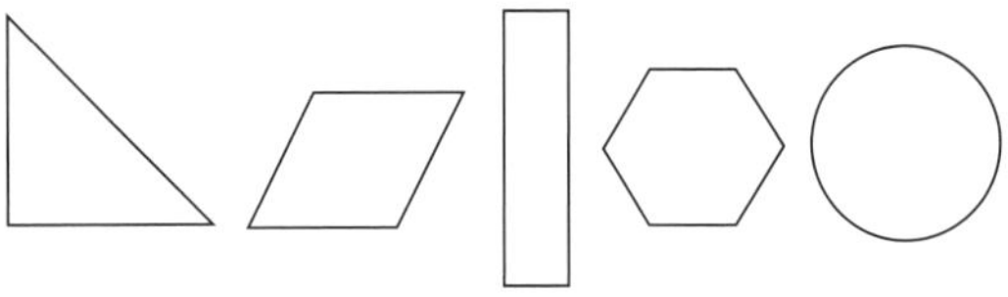

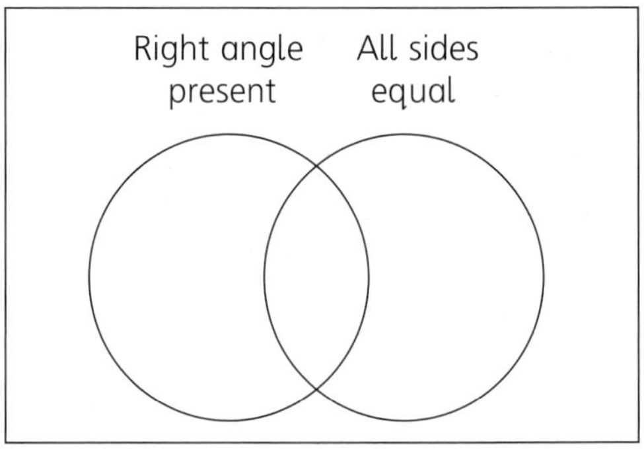

3 Create a tally to show the number of class birthdays in each month.

4 Think about how your school sit in the hall for assembly. How could you present the information as a graph?

5 Add these numbers to the Carroll diagram.

131 120 40 80 75 36 18 25 4 135 9 57

	Even	Odd
Multiple of 5		
Not a Multiple of 5		

1 Teacher's Notes

What sort of sport do other children in the class play? Consider how to go about finding and gathering this information. Present your findings in a table. Ask children to limit their findings to just five kinds of sport.

Children should have discussed the different kinds of sport, asked how many children play each type and written the information into a table. Numbers will vary from class to class.

Present your findings in a bar chart.

2 Teacher's Notes

Complete this Venn diagram by sorting out this set of 2-d shapes. Check the worksheets to see that children have placed the shapes correctly.

Children should have placed the shapes in the correct part of the Venn diagram.

Draw a shape that could fit into the central part of the Venn diagram.

3 Teacher's Notes

Read out a list of birthdays of children in the class. *Create a tally to show the number of birthdays in each month.* Some children may start with their own birthday month while others may start with the current month, or with January. Check that they have been systematic in their tallying.

Children should have a completed tally chart. The order of months should follow the calendar year.

Write two sentences about the information you have gathered.

4 Teacher's Notes

Think about how the children in your school sit in the hall for assembly. Each row has children from a particular class, some rows are longer than others. Could you present this information in a graph? What would it look like? Construct a graph of the seating in assembly.

Children may have suggested a variety of presentations and these will form a useful starting point for discussion.

Which row has the most children in it? Which class is this? Do any rows have exactly the same number of children in? Which classes are these?

5 Teacher's Notes

This is a Carroll diagram showing a way to sort out these numbers. Add the numbers to the chart. Check the worksheets to see that sorting has been done correctly.

Children should put the numbers in the relevant box on the Carroll diagram.

Think of a 3-digit number that could go into each of the boxes on the diagram.

Unit 25

Name ______________________________

1 Put these numbers in order and explain the order you have chosen.

1121 1132 1097 1034 1041 1777

2 Estimate the number that the arrow is pointing to.

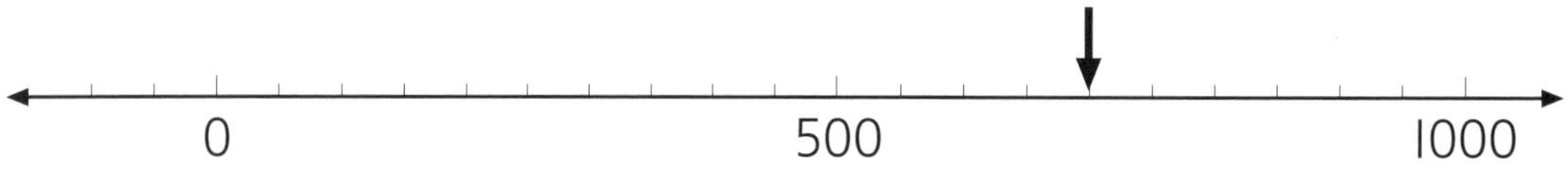

3 Jamie has 3 boxes of multi-base equipment. Which has the greatest value?

4 Chlöe wanted to work out 95 x 11 on her calculator. She entered 12 instead of 11. By how much was she wrong?

5 Here are the results of the welly-throwing competition. Put the results in order, winner first.

10·7 m 15·0 m
0·9 m 0·5 m
2·0 m

5

Place-value, ordering, rounding and reading numbers from scales

1 Teacher's Notes

Put these numbers in order, explaining the order that you have chosen. Many children will make a list of smallest to largest. Some may try the reverse but make sure they are consistent in either case.

Different answers possible, one way would be smallest to largest: 1034, 1041, 1097, 1121, 1132, 1777.

Look back at the original list. Can you sort it into two categories? Can this be done in different ways? Share ideas with a partner.

2 Teacher's Notes

Estimate the number that the arrow is pointing to. Make sure that children make full use of the information given by the number line.

700

Show where these numbers are: three hundred, four hundred, two hundred and fifty. Explain how you made decisions about where to place the numbers. What did you already know? What did you need to work out?

3 Teacher's Notes

Jamie has been given different boxes of multi-base equipment. Which box has the greatest value? Some children may try and answer this straight away. If they get it wrong then encourage them to look closely at the artwork again.

412 ones has the greatest value. Children may assume that 'ones' will always be a smaller amount than 'hundreds', etc – look out for this misconception.

Write these numbers in order from smallest to largest: sixty-three tens, sixty-three ones, sixty-three hundreds. Now come up with three similar numbers of your own for a partner to order.

4 Teacher's Notes

Chlöe wanted to work out ninety-five times eleven on her calculator. Instead of entering eleven she entered twelve. By how much was the answer wrong? Ask children to explain their answer to a friend in class.

Chöe's answer was wrong by 1 x 95.

By how much would Chlöe be wrong if she entered ninety-five times twenty-one instead of ninety-five times eleven? (10 x 95 = 950)

5 Teacher's Notes

Here are the results from a welly-throwing competition. Put the results in order from the longest length to the shortest length so that Mr Brain can hand out the winning rosettes. The winner is the one who threw the longest length.

15·0 m, 10·7 m, 2·0 m, 0·9 m, 0·5 m.

Imagine that the competitors felt extra strong and each one managed to throw the welly twice their original distance. Will the order stay the same or will there be a different winner? Can you explain your answer?

Unit 26

Name ____________________

1 Read the questions out to your partner and give them 10 seconds to answer each one.

41 + 25   99 + 34

66 + 19   89 + 25

2 Answer these questions in words.

a What do you add to 17 to get 25?

b What is 60 take away 19?

c What is 170 less than 250?

3 You know that 50 + 50 = 100. How can you use this to work out 58 + 62?

4 In what year will you have your 99th birthday?

5 What is Ellen's number?

My secret number is a whole number between 1 and 10. If you double it and add 4 you get an odd number.

C Understanding addition and subtraction

1 Teacher's Notes

Read the problems out to your partner and give them only ten seconds to work out the answer to each one. Can they complete all the questions in the given time? Ask children to explain to their partner what strategy they need to do the sums.

66, 85, 133, 114.

Ask children to explain how they obtained their answers. All of the questions lend themselves to an adjustment strategy.

2 Teacher's Notes

How would you tackle these calculations? Describe what you do. Ask children to say aloud how they would do the calculations.

a count on from 17 to 25 = 8.
b subtract 20 then add 1 = 41.
c use the first question to help find the difference between 170 and 250, or count up in tens to 200 then on to 50 = 80.

Think of a calculation that could be solved by using knowledge of doubles and near doubles.

3 Teacher's Notes

You know that fifty plus fifty equals one hundred. How can you use this information to work out fifty-eight plus sixty-two? Ask children to describe the full calculation showing how they have used the information given in the question.

The answer is 20 more (8 + 12) than the answer for 50 + 50.

How can you use the fact that fifty plus fifty equals one hundred to work out fifty-three plus forty-six?

The main point to grasp is that it is possible to break up a complicated addition into smaller parts to make it easier. Ask the children to make up their own examples too.

4 Teacher's Notes

In what year will you have your ninety-ninth birthday? Since answers will vary ask children to do their calculations individually and then ask them what method they used to get their answer.

Answers will vary. To find the answer, add 100 years to the year of birth and subtract 1. Need to adjust for the change of century too.

In which year will you celebrate your fiftieth birthday?

5 Teacher's Notes

Ellen says that her secret number is a whole number between one and ten. If you double it and add four you get an odd number. What could the number be? Explain your answer. This is a reasoning type question. Make sure children understand why it will never be an odd number.

It is impossible. The double of any number is even. If you then add four you still have an even number.

Write a sentence that explains what happens when odd and even numbers are doubled, or when they are multiplied by each other. You will need to test out a few numbers to make sure that your sentence is correct.

Unit 27

Name ____________________

1 You are selling ice cream and have 3 customers buying different ice creams as shown on the table. Each one gives you £1. What change will you give?

Ice Cream	
Single scoop	42p
Wafer	61p
Double scoop	89p

2 Here is the menu for a pizza restaurant. You have £10 and the restaurant doesn't give change. Choose a meal that costs as much of your £10 as possible.

Pizzas		**Extras**		**Drinks**	
Pepperoni	£8·50	Olives	£1·50	Soda	£0·80
Mushroom	£6·68	Hummus	£2·50	Orange Juice	£1·00
Cheese	£5·42	Garlic Bread	£1·05	Lemonade	£0·65

3 Sabrina has 10p. Can she have 7 coins?

4 Make up a real life story using the amount £7·36.

5 Eliot was given £10 from his relatives. £2·50 was from his grandma. What fraction was this? How much money did his other relatives give him?

—
5

Money and 'real life' problems, making decisions and checking results

1 Teacher's Notes

You are selling ice cream and have three customers. Each customer hands you £1 but they buy different ice creams. What change will you give? Children should do the subtraction first on their own. They can then use calculations to check their results.

58p, 39p, 11p.

List the coins you would give each customer in their change. Give out the fewest possible coins to each customer.

2 Teacher's Notes

Here is the menu for a local pizza restaurant. You have £10 to spend on your meal and the restaurant doesn't give change. Choose items to buy that will cost as much of your £10 as possible. Encourage children to think of different combinations of food. They should also think about how the choice of one item will affect how much they can spend on other items.

A mushroom pizza, hummus and soda will be £6·68 + £2·50 + £0·80 = £9·98. Other answers are possible too. Encourage children to explore different combinations.

Choose one pizza, one accompaniment and one drink of your choice. How much does it cost you?

3 Teacher's Notes

Sabrina has 10p. Could she possibly have seven coins? Before using coins to check, children could try and think of the answer by recalling the kinds of coins available and making different combinations of them.

No. It is not possible to make 10p with 7 coins.

Could she possibly have one coin?* (Yes) *How about two coins? Three? Four?

yes

4 Teacher's Notes

Make up a real life story using the amount £7·36. Encourage children to be creative. They could break up the amount into two or three parts too.

There are many possible stories, for example, 'My mum spent £5 on petrol to top up her petrol tank and £2·36 to buy milk and eggs for breakfast. That makes a total of £7·36.'

Make up a real life story that uses: $\frac{3}{4}$***, 1·5, 12.***

5 Teacher's Notes

For Eliot's birthday he received £10 from his relatives. £2·50 of it was from his grandma. What fraction of his birthday money came from Grandma? How much money came from other relatives?

$\frac{1}{4}$ from Grandma, 7·50 from other relatives.

Eliot's brother received £12 in total, and again one quarter of it was given by Grandma. Did she give him the same amount of money as she gave Eliot? **(No, she gave him £3)**

Unit 28

Name ______________________

1 Draw this glass half full.

2 Draw a rectangle with an area of 12 square units.

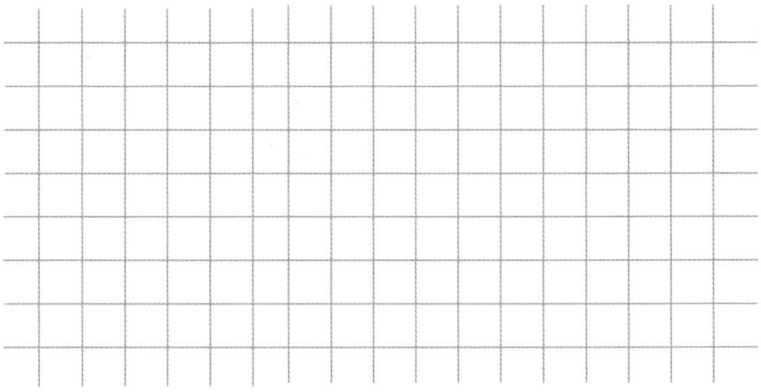

3 The football match started at 2:30pm. They played 45 minutes in each half with a 15 minute break. What time did the match finish?

4 The leisure centre shut for repairs on Friday 14th June. It opened again on Friday the 19th July. For how many weeks was it closed?

5 A class go on a school trip. The coach stops so they can have a meal after 285 miles. The whole journey is 445 miles. How far have they still to go?

5

Measures, including problems

1 Teacher's Notes

This sort of glass is called a schooner. Show it half full of liquid. For this problem children need to do some approximation about how the glass would look half-full. Ask them to explain their sketch.

Children are likely to draw the fluid level half-way between the top and bottom of the glass. Point out that the top is wider than the bottom.

Investigate with the children to find other containers where the half-way mark is not where they would expect it.

2 Teacher's Notes

Draw a rectangle whose area is twelve square units. Children need to first calculate the length of the sides. Make sure they know that there is more than one answer. Extra squared paper may be needed.

The possible rectangles are 1 x 12, 2 x 6, and 3 x 4.

Which of the possible rectangles with area of twelve square units will also have the shortest perimeter?

3 Teacher's Notes

The football match started at 2:30pm. They played forty-five minutes in each half with a fifteen minute break. What time did the match finish? Make sure that children remember that an hour has sixty, not hundred, minutes.

The game ended at 4:15pm.

Five goals were scored in the match and the final score was 1–4. If three goals were scored in the first half, what could the half time scores have been? **(1-2, or 0-3)**

4 Teacher's Notes

The leisure centre shut for repairs on Friday 14th June. It opened again on Friday 19th July. For how many weeks was the leisure centre closed? A month has roughly 4-5 weeks. The closed period is a bit more than a month. Check the estimates using a calendar.

5 weeks.

Usually the leisure centre makes two hundred and sixty-seven pounds profit during each week that it is open. How much money was lost during this closure time? **(£1335)**

It will be quite useful for children to look at a calendar and learn more about how days, weeks and months add up to make a year.

5 Teacher's Notes

A class of children go on a school trip. They travel on the coach, and stop for a meal after two hundred and eighty-five miles. The journey is four hundred and forty five miles. How much further do they have to go? Ask children to explain their calculations and check them.

160 miles to go.

If they are travelling at speeds of forty miles per hour, how much longer will the journey take? **(4 hours)**

Unit 29

Name ____________________

1 Draw this shape when it has been rotated 90° clockwise.

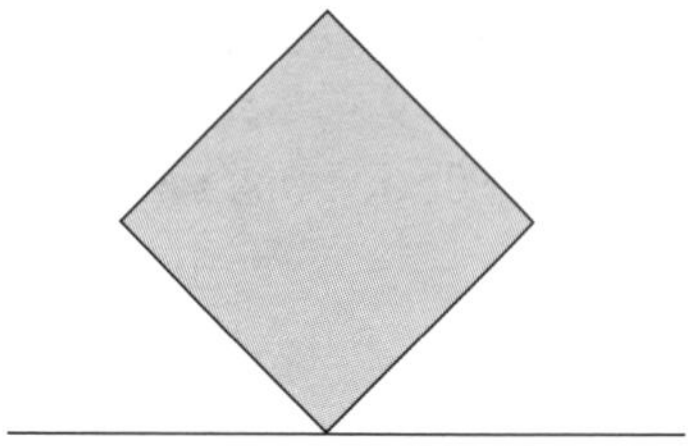

2 There is treasure hidden 2 squares from the X. Where will it be?

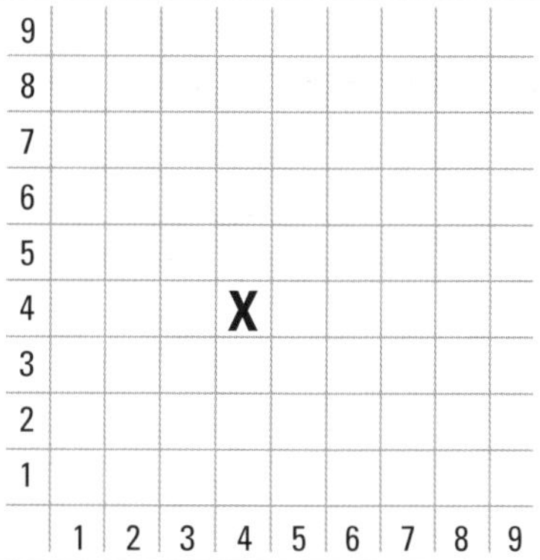

3 Sit back to back with a partner. One of you secretly draws a diagram and describes it to the other, who draws it on his or her paper. Are your drawings the same?

4 Can these three dots be three corners of a square? Explain your thinking.

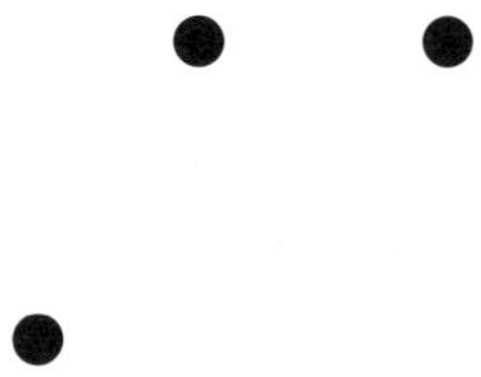

5 A pentagon can be split into 3 triangles each with total inside angles of 180°. So the total inside angles of a pentagon are 3 x 180° = 540°.
Find the total inside angles of these shapes.

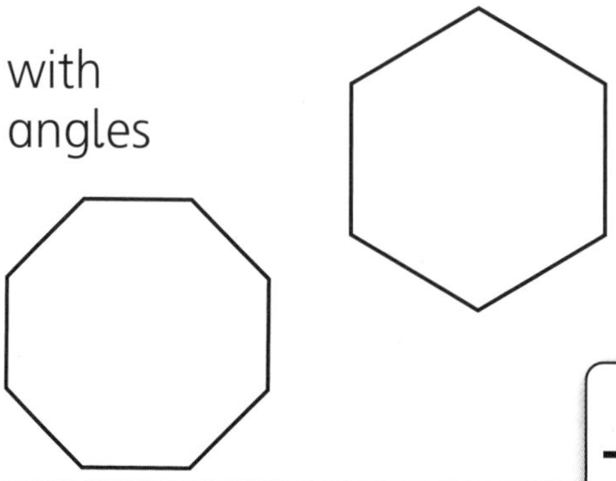

5

Shape and space, reasoning about shapes

1 Teacher's Notes

Draw this shape when it has been rotated ninety degrees clockwise. If children find this difficult they can rotate their pupil page by 90° and see what the shape looks like.

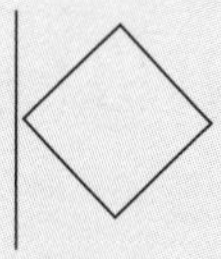

Draw the shape after it has been rotated one hundred and eighty degrees.

2 Teacher's Notes

Imagine that there is some treasure hidden at a grid point two units from the point shown. Show where it might be.

It is not possible to find the exact spot as there can be more than one point that is 2 squares away from the X.

Show all the points that are three units from the original point.

Observe to see which children are better at describing the image, and which are better at listening and visualising the image being described. Ask them to practice using different examples.

3 Teacher's Notes

One of you secretly draws a diagram. Work in pairs. Sit back-to-back with your partner. The one who has drawn the diagram describes it to their partner who must draw it on the same sort of paper. Compare your drawings – they should be the same! Then swap roles.

Answers will vary.

Describe a 2-d shape to a partner so that they can draw it and/or guess which shape it is. Remember to talk about the number of sides, side length, number of corners, size of the angles in the corners, lines of symmetry and so on.

4 Teacher's Notes

Is it possible that these three dots are the corners of a square? Explain your thinking. Allow children to elaborate on their answers. They should give a mathematical explanation for their reply.

No. The layout of these three dots does not create a right angle. For the shape to be a square, each corner must be a right angle.

What might the shape be? Decide on a shape name then complete the diagram to make your shape. Were you right? How many different shapes could it have been?

5 Teacher's Notes

A pentagon can be split into three triangles. Each triangle has total inside angles of one hundred and eighty degrees, so the pentagon must have total inside angles of three times one hundred and eighty degrees = five hundred and forty degrees. Use this method to find the total inside angles of these shapes. Children could start by drawing all the triangles that lie within each shape.

Inside angles of a hexagon = 720 degrees.
Inside angles of an octagon = 1080 degrees.

Do you think this method works with any shape? How could you find out?

Ask children what each angle will be in the regular pentagon, hexagon and octagon. They need to divide the total inside angles by the number of vertices.

Unit 30

Name ____________________

1 Estimate the size of this angle. Use your knowledge of right angles to help you.

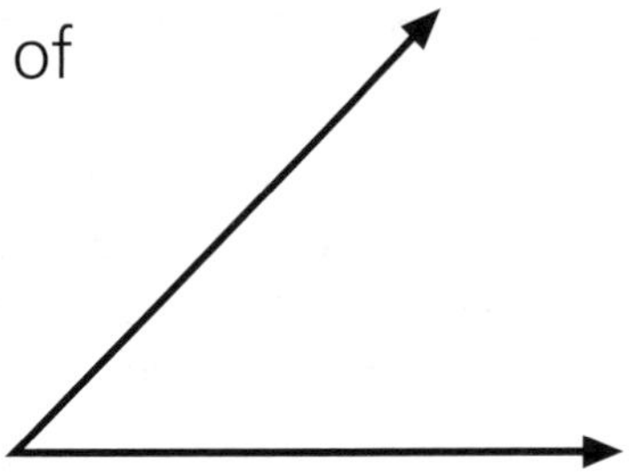

2 Here is a clock reflected in a mirror. What time does it show?

3 Harriet has cut this shape out of the paper. What will it look like when she unfolds it?

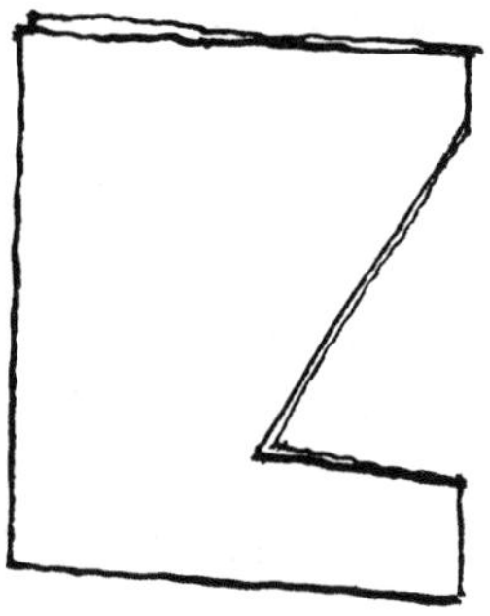

4 What angle is made by the hands of this clock?

5 Plot these points on the grid: (1,1) (3,1) (1,3) (3,3)
Join them to make a shape. What shape have you drawn?

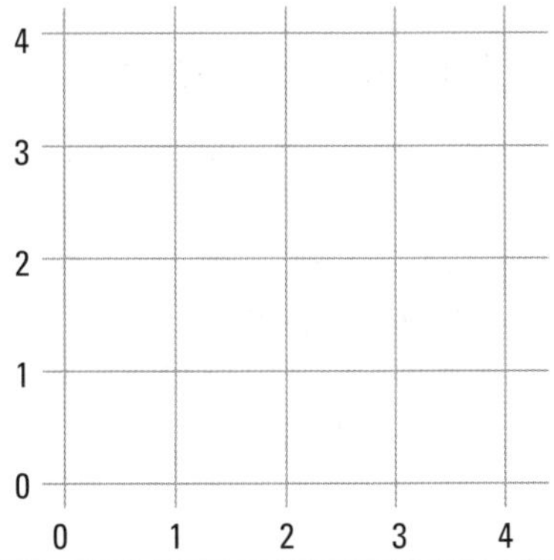

Shape and space, reasoning about shapes

UNIT 30

1 Teacher's Notes

Estimate the size in degrees of this angle. Use your knowledge of right angles to help you. Children need to see that the angle is exactly half of a right angle. Use protractors to check estimates.

The size of the angle is 45 degrees.

Make a right angle tester from a piece of paper (fold it in half and in half again to get a right angle) then fold the right angle exactly in half to make an angle of forty-five degrees. Use this to search round the classroom for angles greater or smaller than forty-five degrees.

2 Teacher's Notes

Here is a clock as seen in a mirror. Can you tell what time it is? If some children struggle with this ask them to re-draw the clock as seen from the front. They need to concentrate on the numbers the hands are pointing to.

Five minutes to 9 o'clock.

Write down your initials. What would they look like if they were seen in a mirror?

3 Teacher's Notes

Harriet is going to cut this shape out of the paper and then unfold it. Draw what the shape will look like when it is unfolded. The fold will act as a line of symmetry in the shape. Children should realise this and draw the second half of the original shape laterally inversed.

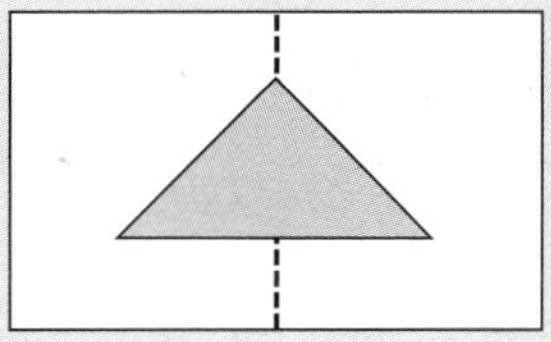

Fold a piece of paper and draw an outline on it. Ask a friend to predict the shape you will get if you cut along the outline and open the shape up.

4 Teacher's Notes

What angle is made by the hands of this clock? This question should help children to think about right angles in different contexts. They might suggest some other times when the clock hands are at 90 degrees.

90 degrees.

What angle is made by the hands of a clock at six o'clock?
(2 right angles = 180 degrees)

5 Teacher's Notes

Plot the points on the grid. Join the points to make a shape. What shape have you drawn? Ask children to confirm their answers by going over the properties of the shape they suggest and checking it against the actual figure.

You have drawn a square.

Draw a triangle on the grid and list the coordinates for each corner of the triangle.

Unit 31

Name ________________________________

1 Look at the symbols. What is the value of this combination?

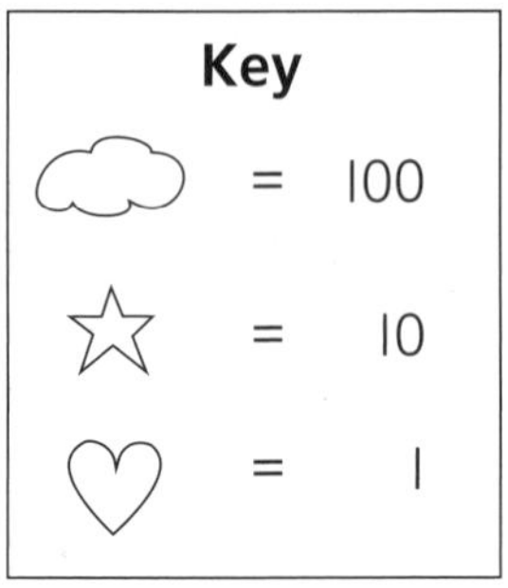

2 Every 4th bead is black. What colour is bead 257? How can you predict this without drawing all the beads?

3 What is this number?

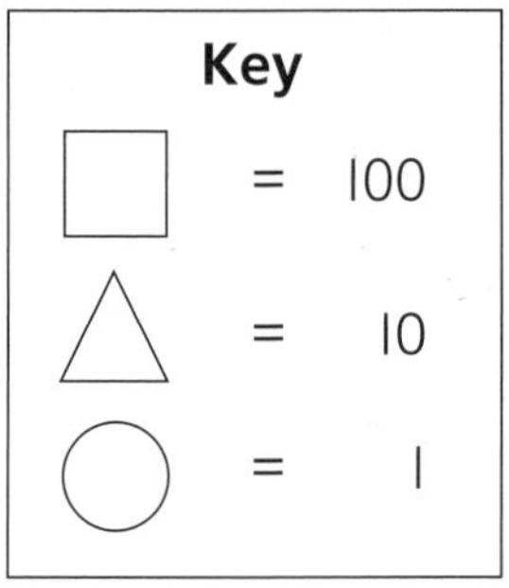

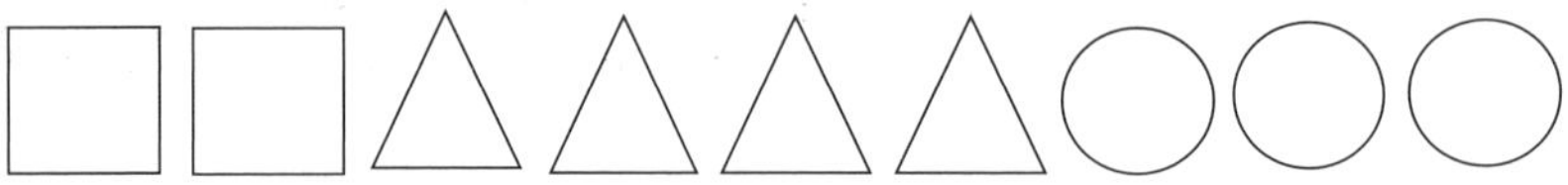

4 I am the multiple of 7 that is closest to 100. Who am I?

5 Write the first 10 multiples of 9. What do you notice?

5

Properties of numbers, number sequences and reasoning about numbers

1 Teacher's Notes

Look at your worksheets. Each symbol has the value shown. What is the value of this combination. Here children need to grasp that these shapes are representing a numerical value each and thus they can add up like ordinary numbers to give a numerical sum.

332

What is the value of these? **(101, 21, 210)**

2 Teacher's Notes

Every fourth bead on this string is black. If the pattern goes from one to one thousand, what colour is bead number two hundred and fifty-seven? Is there a way to predict this rather than drawing out all the beads or writing out all the numbers that would be black?

257 is white. Dividing 257 by 4 shows that 256 is a black bead so 257 will be white.

What colour are bead numbers: one hundred and thirty-four, one hundred, one hundred and seventy-five, one hundred and ninety-one? **(White, black, white, white)**

3 Teacher's Notes

Look at your worksheets. Each symbol has the value shown on the key. Write the value of the number shown by two squares, four triangles and three circles.

243

Write two hundred and thirty-four using the symbols given.

(□ □ △ △ △ ○ ○ ○ ○)

Ask children to make up their own questions using the key and quiz their partners.

4 Teacher's Notes

I am the multiple of seven that is closest to one hundred. Who am I? Ask children how they would work this out. One method is to divide 100 by 7 and subtract the remainder (2) from 100.

98

If I am the multiple of seven closest to two hundred, who am I? **(203) Ask children how they arrived at their answers. One method is to work out 7 x 30, which is 210, then go back 7.**

5 Teacher's Notes

Write the first ten multiples of nine. What patterns do you see? Children may need to be prompted to look at the digits of the multiples to find a sequence.

9,18, 27, 36, 45, 54, 63, 72, 81, 90. One pattern is the tens digit increasing by 1 and the ones digit decreasing by 1 at each step. Children may also notice that the two digits together add up to 9.

Add up the digits of each multiple of nine. What do you notice? **(They all add to give 9.)** ***How could this be used when predicting whether numbers are multiples of nine or not? Are these multiples of nine?*** **Suggest numbers such as 126, 234, 152, 513, 610.**

Unit 32

Name ______________________________

1 Which of these are doubles of whole numbers? Devise a quick way to find out.

151 176 198 205

2 35 ÷ 4 gives a remainder of 3. Find 3 other numbers that also give a remainder of 3 when divided by 4.

3 Is 72 divisible by 3? How can you work this out? Are these numbers divisible by 3?

18 34 26 30 21

4 Estimate the answers to these divisions.

51 ÷ 10 **623 ÷ 10** **847 ÷ 10**

5 How can 10 x 13 be used to help you work out 9 x 13 and 11 x 3? Use words, jottings and diagrams to explain.

/5

Understanding multiplication and division

1 Teacher's Notes

Which of these are doubles of whole numbers? Can you devise a quick test that can be used to find out? Some children may know the answer already. Allow the others to catch up and then make them explain their reasoning.

176 and 198 are doubles. If they are even numbers then they are doubles of other whole numbers.

Give children some numbers and ask which are doubles of doubles.

2 Teacher's Notes

Thirty-five divided by four gives a remainder of three. Work out three other numbers that also give a remainder of three when they are divided by four. One method is to calculate multiples of 4 and add 3 to each of them.

39, 43 , 47 and 51 are some of the possible numbers.

Quickly list five numbers that have no remainders when divided by four. What do we call these numbers? **(Multiples of 4)**

3 Teacher's Notes

Is seventy-two divisible by three? How could you work this out? Do your multiplication tables help? Work out whether these numbers are divisible by three or not. Encourage children to spend some time thinking about the question.

72 is divisible by 3. Children may have worked this out in different ways, for example, a) counting up in 30s (which we know are divisible by 3) to 60, then seeing that 12 are left and 12 is a number divisible by 3; b) adding 7 + 2 = 9 and knowing that 9 is divisible by 3; c) working out the number of 3's in 70 = 23 with 1 remainder, then adding the 1 remainder and the 2 units to make another 3. Allow children time to explain their methods and clarify the strategies you are currently teaching for division.

Twenty-four is divisible by six. Will it also be divisible by three? How do you know?

4 Teacher's Notes

Use your knowledge of the ten times table to help you give an estimated answer (or one with remainders) for these divisions. Children first need to state their estimated answers and then work out the exact answers.

a) a bit more than 5, 5 r1, 5.1.
b) a little more than 60, 62 r 3, 62.3.
c) about 85, 84 r7, 84.7

Give good estimates for: one hundred and five times six; nine hundred and ninety-four times eight, three hundred and ten times eleven.

5 Teacher's Notes

Explain how ten times thirteen can be used to help you work out nine times thirteen and eleven times thirteen. Use words, jottings and diagrams to help you explain in writing.

We know that 10 lots of 13 = 130. To work out nine lots of 13 we subtract one lot of 13: 130 – 13 = 117. To work out 11 lots of 13 we add another one lot of 13: 130 + 13 = 143.

Here is a known fact: fifteen times twenty-four equals three hundred and sixty. Can you use this to work out sixteen times twenty-four and fourteen times twenty-four?

Unit 33

Name ________________

1 One box holds 8 cakes. How many boxes would you need for 124 cakes?

2 How would you cut a rope into 4 equal pieces you had no way of measuring?

3 This box holds 12 sweets. How many ways can 12 sweets be packed into a rectangular box?

4 Three friends paid £24 each for concert tickets. The concert was postponed, and half the money was sent back to them. How much was sent back?

5 You save 10p on Monday, double that on Tuesday, and double again everyday. How much do you have by Sunday?

5

Money and 'real life' problems, making decisions and checking results

UNIT 33

1 Teacher's Notes

One box holds eight cakes. How many boxes do you need for one hundred and twenty-four cakes? As the answer to the division is not a whole number children need to round it up to the next highest whole number.

✔ 16 boxes.

➔ ***How many boxes do you need for this many cakes: forty-seven, thirty-nine, one hundred?***

2 Teacher's Notes

Imagine a friend has a piece of rope and no way of measuring. He wants to cut the rope into four equal pieces (quarters). How can this be done? Explain to a friend. It would be useful to allow children to try this out manually as well, using lengths of thread or rope.

✔ Fold the rope so that you hold the two ends in your left hand and have the middle of the rope in your right hand. Cut the rope at the middle point so it is in half. Then fold one of the 'halves' of the piece of rope in half again and cut. Repeat with the other 'half' and you will have 4 pieces equal in length.

➔ ***Use the 'half and half again' method to work out what a quarter of these numbers is: sixteen, thirty-six, twenty-eight, twenty-five.***

3 Teacher's Notes

Here is a box holding twelve sweets. How many ways can twelve sweets be packed in a rectangular box? The box can be different sizes but it must always be a rectangle.

✔ The sweets could be packed in rows of 1 x 12, 2 x 6, and 3 x 4.

➔ ***List all the possibilities for packing twenty-four sweets in a rectangular box.***

4 Teacher's Notes

Three friends paid £24 each for concert tickets. The show was postponed because the singer had lost his voice, and half the money from each ticket was returned to them. How much in total was returned? Ask children to show their workings on paper and check their answer.

✔ Half of £24 is £12. There were 3 tickets so 3 x £12 = £36 was returned.

➔ ***The tickets were paid for in cash. What did this consist of?* (£20 note, £10 note, £5 note and a £1 coin is one possible solution.)**

5 Teacher's Notes

If you save 10p on the first day of the week, and double that on the second day, and double on the third day, etc. how much will you have saved by the end of the week? This question requires children to generate a sequence where every new number is twice as much as the previous number.

✔ Day 1 = 10p. Day 2 = 20p. Day 3 = 40p. Day 4 = 80p. Day 5 = £1·60. Day 6 = £3·20. Day 7 = £6·40. Total savings = £12·70.

➔ ***If I save this much each week, after how many weeks will I have saved over £50?* (4 weeks = £50·80)**

Unit 34

Name ______________________

1 Terry has 4 m of string. He wants to cut it into 35 cm lengths to tie up his plants. How many plants can he tie up?

2 Think of a single digit number. Double it. Add 4. Halve it. Subtract 2. What number did you finish on? Explain how this works.

3 What fraction of these footballs are inside the ring? How do you express this as a decimal?

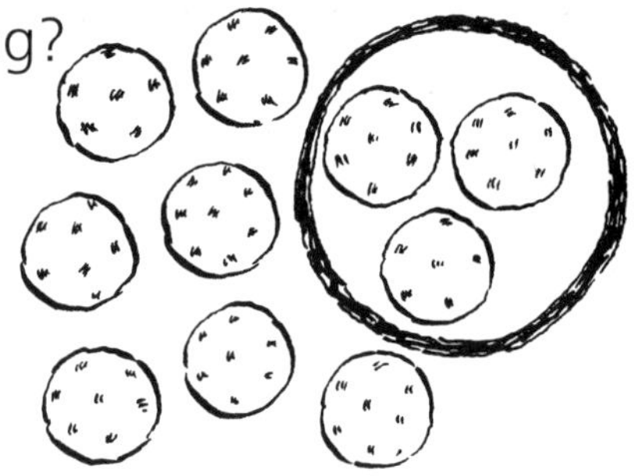

4 Here are 2 bottles of juice. What fraction of the large bottle is the small bottle equal to?

5 Mrs Evans spends 2 days a week at home. How many days will she spend at home in 8 weeks?

5

Fractions and decimals

1 Teacher's Notes

Terry has a long piece of string measuring four metres. He wants to use it in the garden to tie plants onto support sticks. Each plant will need thirty-five centimetres of string. How many plants can he tie up? Ask children to answer the question fully, also accounting for the remainder in the division.

11 strips of 35 cm = 385 cm. He can tie up 11 plants and will have 15 cm of string left.

He decides instead to only use twenty centimetres for each plant and can now tie up more plants. How many more can he tie up? **(He can tie up 20 plants so the answer is 9 plants more. Make sure children answer the question rather than leaving their working out at 20 plants.)**

2 Teacher's Notes

Think of a single digit number. Double it. Add four. Halve it. Subtract two. What number did you finish on? Try this a few times and then try to work out and explain why it works each time. Ask children to try this with odd and even numbers.

Whatever number is chosen, the double will be an even number. 4 is added to it and the answer is still an even number. This means that when it is halved it remains a whole number. Only 2 is subtracted because the original 4 which was added on has now been halved. This should take you back to the original number.

Make up another number chain that finishes on the same number that you started on, and that involves doubling and halving. Give it to a friend to try out.

3 Teacher's Notes

What fraction of these footballs are inside the ring? Can you think of a way to express this as a decimal?

$\frac{3}{10}$, three tenths, 0·3.

Circle eight tenths. How many footballs is this? **(8)**

4 Teacher's Notes

Here are two bottles of juice. Compare the sizes of the two bottles. What fraction of the large bottle is the small bottle equal to? To work out the fraction children need to divide the smaller quantity by the larger quantity.

One quarter, because 250 ml is $\frac{1}{4}$ of 1000 ml.

If you had seven small bottles, how many large bottles would that be equal to? **(1 and $\frac{3}{4}$ large bottles)**

5 Teacher's Notes

Every week Mrs Evans spends two days at home (Saturday and Sunday). So in every two weeks she spends four days at home. How many days will she spend at home in eight weeks? Children may get confused if they convert weeks into days. They do not need to do that conversion for this question.

In 8 weeks Mrs Evans will spend 16 days at home.

The autumn term at school is twelve weeks long. How many days will Mrs Evans spend at home? **(24 days)**

Unit 35

Name ____________________

1 Which of these is always true, whatever number A is?

$A + 9 = 9$

$A + 0 = 0$

$A + 0 = A$

2 Sunita saw the doctor on June 15th. She was told to come back in 2 weeks. When was her next appointment?

3 Emily says that she has lived 5000 days. Is this possible?

4 Using each of these numbers once: 1, 2, 3, 4 and any of these signs: +, -, x , ÷, can you make each number from 1 to 40?

5 Work out the missing digits in these number sentences.

4_6 + _32 = 758

8_ + _1 = 130

_73 − 2_1 = 332

5

Mental calculation strategies and pencil and paper procedures

UNIT 35

1 Teacher's Notes

Which of the following is always true regardless of the value for A? Children could test these statements using number examples but they should gradually arrive at the actual principles behind these numerical relations.

✓ A + 0 = A

➔ ***What answer do you get when you multiply a number by zero?***

2 Teacher's Notes

Sunita had a doctor's appointment on June 15. The doctor said, 'Come back in another two weeks'. When was Sunita's new appointment? This question requires keeping in mind the number of days in a week and in a month.

✓ Add another 14 days onto June 15 = June 29.

➔ ***What would the date be if the doctor had said, 'Come back in four weeks?'*** **(July 13)**

3 Teacher's Notes

Emily says that she has lived five thousand days. Is this possible? There are 365 days in a year. Make sure children do the division correctly. They need to find out what 5000 days is equivalent to in years.

✓ Yes. 5000 days is about $13\frac{1}{2}$ years.

➔ ***Could someone in your town have lived fifty thousand days?*** **(No. 50,000 days is about 135 years.)**

4 Teacher's Notes

Using each of the numbers one, two, three and four once and the signs plus, minus, times or divide can you make each number from one to forty? Ask children to try out different combinations and see what numbers they generate.

✓ It is possible – though children need to be inventive and persistent in discovering some of the solutions, e.g. 6 = (3x4) ÷ (1x2). You may simplify the task by not insisting that they use every digit every time.

➔ ***Can you make the number one hundred this way?***

5 Teacher's Notes

Work out the missing digits in these number sentences on your worksheets. Some children might find it helpful to re-write the number sentence vertically so that they can match up the numbers in each position: units, tens, hundreds.

✓ 426 + 332 = 758
89 + 41 = 130
573 – 241 = 332

➔ ***How many possible answers can there be for this one?***
_3_ – 2_ _ = 424.

Unit 36

Name ____________________

1 A is a collection of even numbers from 1 to 10. B is a collection of numbers from 1 to 10. Put the numbers in the right place on the diagram.

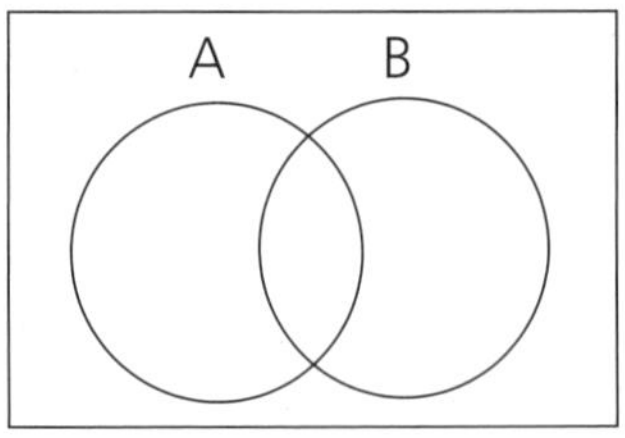

2 Look at the pictogram. How many books have each class read?

 = 5 books

Class 1
Class 2
Class 3
Class 4
Class 5

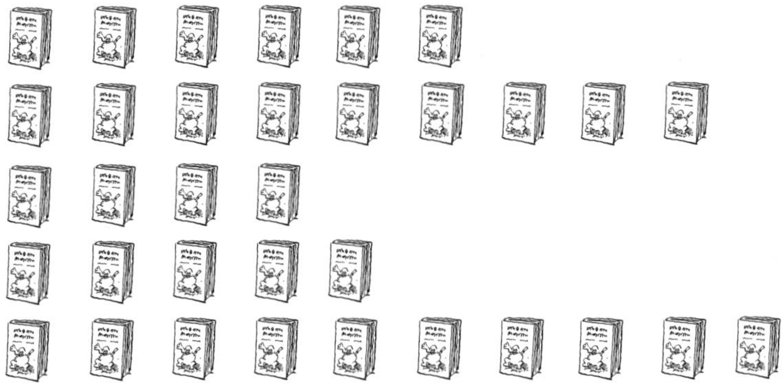

3 Plan how you could find out which teacher has the newest car.

4 Who in the class can jump the furthest? Plan how you could find out. Think about how you would measure, and how to present your results.

5 Construct a Carroll diagram to show this set of data.

Amy	Brown hair	Blue eyes
James	Not brown hair	Blue eyes
Matthew	Brown hair	Not blue eyes
Jenny	Brown hair	Blue eyes
Richard	Not brown hair	Not blue eyes

1 Teacher's Notes

A is a collection of even numbers from one to ten. B is a collection of numbers from one to ten. Put the numbers in the correct place on the diagram.

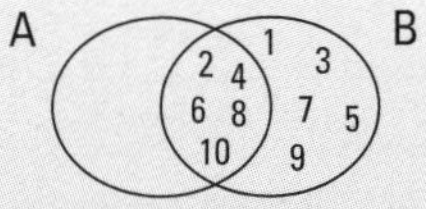

Geoff likes these numbers: 33, 53, 15, 79, 91 and 37. He does not like: 24, 28, 38, 12, 46, and 86. Which of these does he like: 66, 93, 63, 39, 51? **(Geoff likes numbers in which the digits are odd.)**

2 Teacher's Notes

Here is a pictogram showing the number of books read by each class in one month. One picture represents five books. Use the graph to answer these questions: a) which class has read the most books? How many have they read? Why might they have read more? b) Which class has read twenty fewer books than the class that have read the most? c) How many books has Class 2 read? d) If the classes were ordered from largest number of books read to smallest, what would the order be?

a) class 5, 50 books, maybe older
b) class 1
c) 45 books
d) 5, 2, 1, 4, 3.

What is the total number of books read? **(170 books)**

3 Teacher's Notes

Plan how you could find out which teacher has the newest car. Gather the information and present it in a suitable way. Ask children to make a prioritised list of all the things they could do to get the information.

Look at the registration plates, ask the teachers, do a survey… Could be presented as a list – newest to oldest, or in a table.

Would it be appropriate to show your findings in a bar chart? How could this be done? Would it make sense?

4 Teacher's Notes

Which child in the class can jump the furthest? How could you find out? What would you need to do? What would you measure? How would you record it? How would you present your findings? Plan out what you would do at each stage of the investigation.

Discuss strategies and methods suggested.

Choose one appropriate method and carry it out. Present findings in a bar chart. **Discuss the methods used – was it efficient? Are children able to answer the question posed at the start of the investigation?**

5 Teacher's Notes

Construct a Carroll diagram to show this data on the worksheets. These are only two variables with two alternatives each. Encourage children to analyse the data logically, looking for how it could be organised using these variables.

	Brown hair	Not brown hair
Blue eyes	Amy Jenny	James
Not blue eyes	Matthew	Richard

Put yourself and the members of your family onto the Carroll diagram.

Sample medium-plan: Autumn term

Unit	Topic	Objectives; Children will be taught to:	Problem Solving Unit
1	Place value, ordering, rounding Reading numbers from scales	Read and write whole numbers to 10 000 in figures and words. Know what each digit represents and partition into Th H T U. Read and write the vocabulary of estimation. Estimate up to 250 objects. Estimate a proportion (fraction). Read scales to a suitable degree of accuracy.	1
2–3	Understanding + and – Mental calculation strategies (+ and –) Pencil and paper procedures (+ and –)	Consolidate understanding of relationship between addition/subtraction. Understand commutative law of addition. Count on or back in repeated steps of 1, 100, 1000. Identify near doubles. Count up through next multiple of 10, 100, 1000. Use informal pencil and paper methods to support, record or explain addition and subtraction.	2
	Money and 'real life' problems Making decisions, checking results	Convert £ to p. Choose appropriate number operations and calculation methods to solve money or 'real life' word problems with one/two steps. Explain and record methods. Check with addition in a different order.	3
4–6	Measures, including problems	Use, read, write km, m, cm, mm and mile. Know and use relationships between units. Know 1/2, 1/4, 3/4, 1/10 of 1 kilometre in m, 1 metre in cm or mm. Suggest suitable units and equipment to estimate or measure length. Record metres and centimetres using decimals, and other measurements using mixed units. Convert up to 1000 cm to metres and vice versa. Measure/calculate perimeter of rectangles and simple shapes (cm). Choose appropriate number operations and calculation methods to solve measurement word problems with one or more steps. Explain and record methods.	4
	Shape and space	Describe and visualise 3-D and 2-D shapes, inc. tetrahedron, heptagon. Recognise equilateral and isosceles triangles.	5
	Reasoning about shapes	Classify shapes (right angles, regularity, symmetry). Recognise position on square grids with numbered lines. Investigate general statements about shapes.	6
7	**Assess and review**		
8	Properties of numbers and number sequences Reasoning about numbers	Recognise, extend number sequences formed by counting from any number in steps of constant size, e.g. 25 to 500. Recognise odd and even numbers up to 1000 and some of their properties, e.g. sums, differences of pairs of odd/even numbers. Solve number puzzles, recognise patterns, generalise and predict.	7
9–10	Understanding x and ÷ Mental calculation strategies (x and ÷) Pencil and paper procedures (x and ÷)	Extend understanding of x and ÷ and their relationship to each other and to + and –. Use doubling and halving of two-digit numbers, e.g. x4 = double double, x5 = x10 halve, x20 = x10 double, x8 = x4 double, 1/4 = half of one 1/2. Approximating first, use informal pencil and paper methods to multiply and divide.	8
	Money and 'real life' problems Making decisions, checking results	Choose appropriate number operations and calculation methods to solve money and 'real life' word problems with one or more steps. Explain and record methods. Check with equivalent calculation.	9
11	Fractions and decimals	Use fraction notation. Recognise fractions that are several parts of a whole, and mixed numbers. Find fractions of shapes. Relate fractions to division and find simple fractions of quantities.	10
12	Understanding + and – Mental calculation strategies (+ and –) Pencil and paper procedures (+ and –) Time, including problems	Consolidate understanding of subtraction as the inverse of addition. Find a small difference by counting up. Use relationship between + and –. Develop written methods for + and – of whole numbers less than 1000. Use, read, write vocabulary of time. Read time to 1 min on analogue/2-hour digital clock. Use 9:53, a.m. and p.m. Solve time word problems.	11
13	Handling data	Solve a given problem by collecting, classifying, representing and interpreting data in tally charts, frequency tables, pictograms (symbols representing 2, 5, 10 units). Include use of computer.	12
14	**Assess and review**		

C Sample medium-plan: Spring term

Unit	Topic	Objectives; children will be taught to:	Problem Solving unit
1	Place value, ordering, rounding Reading numbers from scales	Multiply and divide an integer up to 1000 by 10: understand the effect. Read and write the vocabulary of comparing and ordering numbers. Use symbols = < > correctly. Give a number lying between two others. Use vocabulary of approximation. Round any positive number less than 1000 to nearest 10. Recognise negative numbers in context: number line, thermometer.	13
2–3	Understanding + and – Mental calculation strategies (+ and –) Pencil and paper procedures (+ and –)	Understand principle (not name) of commutative law for + not –. Add several small numbers by finding pairs that total 10, or 9 or 11. Partition into tens and units, adding tens first. Add three two-digit multiples of 10. Develop/refine written methods for addition/subtraction, including money.	14
	Money and 'real life' problems Making decisions, checking results	Choose appropriate number operations and calculation methods to solve money and 'real life' word problems with one or more steps. Explain working. Check with an equivalent calculation.	15
5–6	Measures, and time, including problems	Estimate and check times using seconds, minutes, hours. Measure and compare using kilograms and grams, and know and use the relationship between them. Know 1/4, 1/2, 3/4 and 1/10 of 1 kg in grams. Suggest suitable units and equipment to estimate or measure mass. Read scales. Record measurements to suitable degree of accuracy, using mixed units, of the nearest whole/half/quarter unit (e.g. 3·25 kg). Measure and calculate area of rectangles and simple shapes, using counting methods and standard units (square centimetres). Choose appropriate number operations and calculation methods to solve measurement word problems with one or more steps. Explain working.	16 17
	Shape and space Reasoning about shapes	Make shapes and discuss properties. Visualise solid shapes from 2-D drawings. Identify simple nets. Recognise clockwise, anti-clockwise. Start to draw, measure and order angles. Use eight compass points. Recognise horizontal and vertical lines. Solve shape problems or puzzles. Explain reasoning and methods.	18
7	**Assess and review**		
8	Properties of numbers and number sequences Reasoning about numbers	Recognise, extend number sequences formed by counting from any number in steps of constant size, extend beyond zero if counting back. Investigate general statements about familiar numbers. Explain methods and reasoning.	19
9–10	Understanding x and ÷ Mental calculation strategies (x and ÷) Pencil and paper procedures (x and ÷)	Understand commutative and associative laws of multiplication. Divide a whole number of £ by 2, 4, 5 or 10 to give £1p. Use closely related facts, e.g. derive x9 or x11 from x10, or derive x8 from x4 plus x2. Partition and multiply. Develop and refine written methods for TU x U.	20
	Money and 'real life' problems Making decisions, checking results	Choose appropriate number operations and calculation methods to solve money and 'real life' word problems with one or more steps. Explain working. Check with inverse operation.	21
11	Fractions and decimals	Recognise equivalence of simple fractions. Identify two fractions with total of 1. Compare a fraction with one half, and say whether it is greater or less. Use decimal notation for tenths, hundredths (money, metres are centimetres) and use in context. Round to the nearest £ or metre Convert £ to p. or metres to centimetres, and vice versa. Order decimals with two places.	22 23
12	Handling data	Solve a given problem by collecting, classifying, representing and interpreting data in bar charts; intervals labelled in 2s, 5s, 10s, 20s. Include use of computer.	24
13	**Assess and review**		

Sample medium-term plan: Summer term

Unit	Topic	Objectives; children will be taught to:	Problem Solving unit
1	Place value, ordering, rounding Reading numbers from scales	Begin to multiply whole numbers by 100. Order a set of whole numbers up to 10000. Round any positive integer to the nearest 10 or 100. Read a variety of scales and dials to a suitable degree of accuracy.	25
2-3	Understanding + and – Mental calculation strategies (+ –) Pencil and paper procedures (+ –)	Understand the principles of associative law for addition (not name). Add or subtract the nearest multiple of 10 and adjust. Use number facts and place value to add/subtract mentally any pair of two-digit whole numbers. Develop, refine written methods for column addition/subtraction. Add more than two whole numbers less than 1000, and money.	26
	Money and 'real life' problems Making decisions, checking results	Choose appropriate operations and calculation methods to solve money and 'real life' word problems with one or more steps. Explain working. Check using knowledge of sums of odd/even numbers.	27
4–6	Measures, including problems	Use, read, write litre (l), millilitre (ml), pint. Know 1/4, 1/2, 3/4, 1/10 of 1 litre in ml. Suggest suitable units and equipment to estimate or measure capacity. Read scales. Record measurements to suitable degree of accuracy, using mixed units, or the nearest whole/half/quarter unit (e.g 3·25 litres). Choose appropriate number operations and calculation methods to solve measurement word problems with one or more steps. Explain working.	28
	Shape and space Reasoning about shapes	Read and begin to write the vocabulary of movement. Make and describe patterns involving translation. Begin to measure angles in degrees. Know whole turn, 360°, 4 right angles; quarter turn, 90°, 1 right angle; half turn, 180°, 2 right angles. Recognise 45° as half a right angle. Sketch reflection of simple shape in a mirror.	29 30
7	**Assess and review**		
8	Properties of numbers And number sequences Reasoning about numbers	Recognise multiples of 2, 3, 4, 5, 10, up to 10th multiple. Solve number problems and puzzles. Explain methods and reasoning orally and in writing.	31
9–10	Understanding x and ÷ Mental calculation strategies (x and ÷) Pencil and paper procedures (x and ÷)	Understand distributive law. Round up or down after division. Use relation between x and ÷. Use known facts to multiply and divide. Develop and refine written methods for TU ÷ U	32
	Money and 'real life' problems Making decisions, checking results	Choose appropriate operations and calculation methods to solve money and 'real life' word problems with one or more steps. Explain working. Check results by approximating.	33
11	Fractions and decimals	Begin to use ideas of simple properties. Recognise the equivalence of decimal, fraction forms of one half, one quarter and tenths.	34
12	Understanding + and – Mental calculation strategies (+ and –) Pencil and paper procedures Time including problems	Consolidate understanding of addition and subtraction. Add/subtract mentally any pair of two-digit whole numbers. Refine column addition and subtraction. Read timetables and use this year's calendar. Solve problems involving time.	35
13	Handling data	Solve a given problem by collecting, classifying, representing and interpreting data in Venn and Carroll diagrams: two criteria. Use a computer and a branching tree program to sort shapes or numbers.	36
14	**Assess and review**		

Class:

Name	Unit																																		
	1	2	3	4	5	6	7	8	9	10	11	12	13	14	15	16	17	18	19	20	21	22	23	24	25	26	27	28	29	30	31	32	33	34	35	36

Individual Record Sheet

Name: **Term:**

Unit	Comment